D1196438

OTHER LEGAL HUMOR
FROM CATBIRD PRESS

By Arnold B. Kanter, Illustrated by Paul Hoffman

Was That a *Tax* Lawyer Who Just Flew Over?
The Ins & Outs of Law Firm Mismanagement
Advanced Law Firm Mismanagement
The Handbook of Law Firm Mismanagement

Edited by Daniel R. White

Trials & Tribulations: Appealing Legal Humor
(an anthology of the best in legal humor)

THE BREATH OF AN UNFEE'D LAWYER

SHAKESPEARE ON LAWYERS AND THE LAW

Edited by Edward J. Bander

Illustrated by Jerry Warshaw

Catbird Press

CATBIRD PRESS, 16 Windsor Road, North Haven, CT 06473
800-360-2391, catbird@pipeline.com.
If you like this book and would like to see what else
we publish, please write, call, or e-mail us for our
catalog. Catbird's legal humor books are
available at special bulk-purchase discounts
for gifts, promotions, and fund-raising.
For details, contact Catbird Press.

Our books are distributed to the trade
by Independent Publishers Group.

To Tema

Library of Congress Cataloging-in-Publication Data
Shakespeare, William, 1564-1616
[Selections. 1996]
The breath of an unfee'd lawyer : Shakespeare on lawyers
and the law / edited by Edward J. Bander ;
illustrated by Jerry Warshaw
ISBN 0-945774-32-X (alk. paper)
1. Shakespeare, William, 1564-1616—Quotations.
2. Lawyers—Quotations, maxims, etc.
3. Law—Quotations, maxims, etc.
4. Quotations, English.   I. Bander, Edward J. II. Title.
PR2892.B25   1996
822.3'3--dc20   96-27864 CIP

A

ABUSE OF PROCESS
A1.02
[A] lily-livered, action-taking knave
King Lear II ii

ACTION AT LAW
A1.04
It is not so; for how can this be true,
That you stand forfeit, being those that sue?
Love's Labour's Lost V ii

See Equitable Life v. Porter-Englehart, 867 F. 2d 79, 88 (1989).
Selya, J.

ACTION ON THE CASE
A1.08
Dromio: I do not know the matter; he is 'rested on
the case.
Adriana: What, is he arrested? Tell me at whose suit.
Dromio: I know not at whose suit he is arrested well;
But he's in a suit of buff which 'rested him,
that can I tell
Comedy of Errors IV ii

ADMINISTRATIVE OFFICIALS
A1.12
[P]elting, petty officer ...
Drest in a little brief authority,
Most ignorant of what he's most assured, ...
Plays such fantastic tricks ...
As makes the angels weep.
Measure for Measure II ii

See Magreta v. Ambassador Steel, 158 N.W. 2d 473, 476
(Mich. 1968). See also Regina v. Horsham Industries [1982] Q.B. 762.

ADVERSARY SYSTEM

A1.16

And do as adversaries do in law,
Strive mightily, but eat and drink as friends.

Taming of the Shrew I ii

Used in the sense of professional responsibility in Gregori v. Bank of
America, 254 Cal. Rptr. 853, 865 (1989) by Kline, J.

A1.20

[T]here's a skirmish of wit between them.

Much Ado About Nothing I i

A1.24

There is nothing either good or bad, but thinking
makes it so.

Hamlet II ii

"But as Shakespeare reminds us in language antedating almost all
our sacred precedent..." See Bronson, J. in Todd v. Rochester
Community Schools, 200 N.W. 2d 90, 98 (Mich. App. 1972).

ADVERSARY SYSTEM (CONT.)

A1.28
[C]onscience does make cowards of us all
Hamlet III i

ADVERTISING LEGAL SERVICES

A1.32
[A] peevish self-will'd harlotry.
1 Henry IV - III i

A1.36
I'll tickle your catastrophe
2 Henry IV - II i

ADVISING A WITNESS
A1.40
Assume a virtue, if you have it not.
Hamlet III iv

AGENCY
A1.42
So, if a son that is by his father sent about merchandise do sinfully miscarry upon the sea, the imputation of his wickedness, by your rule, should be imposed upon his father that sent him
Henry V - IV i

AIDING AND ABETTING
A1.44
How oft the sight of means to do ill deeds
Make ill deeds done!
King John IV ii

ALTERNATIVE ALLEGATIONS, REPLY TO
A1.48
The lady doth protest too much
Hamlet III ii

Very popular with judges in castigating lawyers and their brethren. One example is Harris v. Reeves, 946 F. 2d 214, 226 (1991). Aldisert, J. in dissent.

ALTERNATE DISPUTE RESOLUTION
A1.52
Brutus: Words before blows ...
Octavius: Not that we love words better, as you do.
Brutus: Good words are better than bad strokes, Octavius.
Julius Caesar V i

ALTERNATIVE PLEADING
A1.56
I would I knew in what particular action to try him.
All's Well That Ends Well III vi

AMBULANCE CHASING
A1.64
[L]ike greyhounds in the slips,
Straining upon the start.
Henry V - III i

See Mercer v. Birchman, 510 F. Supp. 99,
105 (1981). Clavie, J.

AMERICAN JUDICIARY SOCIETY
A1.68
[W]e defy augury.
Hamlet V ii

U.S. v. Cox, 464 F. 2d 937, 944 (1972). Rubin, J. Can an
appellate court reason why a defendant pleaded guilty?

AMERICAN LAW REPORTS
A1.72
This fierce abridgement
Hath to it circumstantial branches, which
Distinctions should be rich in.
Cymbeline V v

AMICI CURIAE BRIEFS
A1.76
[A]nd the hand of time
Shall draw this brief into as huge a volume.
King John II i

ANSWERING INTERROGATORIES
A1.80
A night is but small breath and little pause
To answer matters of this consequence.
Henry V - II iv

APPEALS
A1.84
Comedy of Errors [all acts]

A1.86
[M]ake assurance double sure
Macbeth IV i

Jacobs v. Bd. of Edu., 409 N.Y.S. 2d 234, 240 (1978). Shapiro, J. See also Wm. Stevens & Sons v. Conservators [1958] 1 Lloyd's Rep. 401.

APPEALS - DENIED
A1.88
The game is up.
Cymbeline III iii

APPEALS - REMANDING TO LOWER COURT
A1.90
The better part of valor is discretion
1 Henry IV - V iv

APPEALS - UPHELD
A1.92
Roses have thorns, and silver fountains mud;
Clouds and eclipses stain both moon and sun,
And loathsome canker lives in sweetest bud.
All men make faults
Sonnet 35

Mex-Amer. Bar Assn. v. Texas, 755 F. Supp 735, 745 (1990).
Burton, J. analogizes the current state of a law to this sonnet.

APPORTIONMENT
A1.94
Methinks my moiety, north from Burton here,
In quantity equals not one of yours
1 Henry IV - III i

ARBITRATION
A1.98
Queen Isabel: [W]e fairly hope ... that this day
        Shall change all griefs and quarrels into love.
King Henry: To cry amen to that, thus we appear.
Henry V - V ii

A2.00
Let this world no longer be a stage
To feed contention in a lingering act
2 Henry IV - I i

ARBITRATION (CONT.)

A2.02

[B]etter a little chiding than a great deal of heart-break.

Merry Wives of Windsor V iii

ARBITRATOR

A2.04

Wrath-kindled gentlemen, be rul'd by me;
Let's purge this choler without letting blood;
This we prescribe, though no physician;
Deep malice makes too deep incision:
Forget, forgive; conclude and be agreed;
Our doctors say this is no time to bleed.

Richard II - I i

A2.06

I will fit thee with the remedy.

Much Ado About Nothing I ii

ARGUMENTS - REPEATING THEM AGAIN AND AGAIN

A2.08

To gild refined gold, to paint the lily

King John IV ii

Courts keep making the point that this quote is occasionally mangled. Thames v. Maurice Sporting Goods, 686 F. Supp. 208, 215 (1988)

ARREST WARRANT

A2.10

And every word in it a gaping wound,
Issuing life-blood.

Merchant of Venice III ii

ASSAULT

A2.12

Must I give way and room to your rash choler?
Shall I be frighted when a madman stares?
Julius Caesar IV iii

ASSOCIATE - ASKING FOR A RAISE

A2.14

[Y]ou may as well go about to turn the sun to ice
with fanning in [the managing partner's] face with
a peacock's feather.
Henry V - IV i

ASSOCIATE, BECOMING AN

A2.16

To lie in cold obstruction and to rot;
This sensible warm motion to become
A kneaded clod; and the delighted spirit
To bathe in fiery floods, or to reside
In thrilling region of thick-ribbed ice;
To be imprison'd in the viewless winds,
And blown with restless violence round about
The pendent world.
Measure for Measure III i

ASSOCIATES - HOURS

A2.20

We have heard the chimes at midnight
2 Henry IV - III ii

ASSOCIATES - MINGLING WITH SENIOR PARTNER

A2.24

Alonso: I long to hear the story of your life, which
    must take the ear strangely.
Prospero: I'll deliver all
The Tempest V i

ASSOCIATES - PARTNERS' VIEW

A2.28

How sharper than a serpent's tooth it is
To have a thankless child!
King Lear I iv

See Mileski v. Locker, 178 N.Y.S. 2d 911, 917 (1958). Pette, J.

ASSOCIATES - STAYING WITH FIRM
A2.32
[R]ather bear those ills we have
Than fly to others that we know not of?
Hamlet III i

ASSOCIATES - WEEKLY PAYCHECK
A2.36
A crown's worth of good interpretation; there
'tis, boy.
2 Henry IV - II ii

ASSOCIATION OF THE BAR OF THE CITY OF NEW YORK
A2.40
The cloud-capp'd towers, the gorgeous palaces,
The solemn temples
The Tempest IV i

ATTORNEY-CLIENT PRIVILEGE
A2.44
2nd Lord: I will tell you a thing, but you shall let it
    dwell darkly with you.
1st Lord: When you have spoken it, 'tis dead, and
    I am the grave of it.
All's Well That Ends Well IV iii

AUTUMN ON WALL STREET

A2.48

I'll tell you them all by their names as they pass by
Troilus and Cressida I ii

B

BAILIFF
B1.02
I am the besom that must sweep the court clean of
such filth as thou art.
2 Henry VI - IV vii

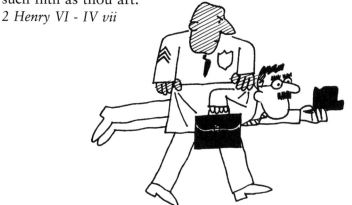

BANKRUPTCY FOLLOWING CLASS ACTION
B1.08
[S]ince I cannot prove a lover ... I am determined to
prove a villain.
Richard III - I i

E. A. Polack v. A.S.A. Bldrs., 534 S.W. 2d 505, 506 (Missouri 1976).
Clemens, J.

BANKRUPTCY LAWYERS - COMPANY'S VIEW
AFTER LIQUIDATION
B1.12
And being fed by us, you us'd us so
As that ungentle gull, the cuckoo's bird,
Useth the sparrow; — did oppress our nest;
Grew by our feeding to so great a bulk.
1 Henry IV - V i

BANKRUPTCY PROCEEDINGS

B1.16
Neither a borrower nor a lender be
Hamlet I iii

In re 64 Columbus Ave., 968 F. 2d 1332, 1335 (1992). Bownes, J.

BAR EXAMINATION

B1.20
There is a tide in the affairs of men
Which, taken at the flood, leads on to fortune;
Omitted, all the voyage of their life
Is bound in shallows and in miseries.
On such a full sea are we now afloat;
And we must take the current when it serves
Or lose our ventures.
Julius Caesar IV iii

B1.24
Bring me to the test
Hamlet III iv

BAR EXAMINATION (CONT.)

B1.28

Double, double, toil and trouble;
Fire burn and cauldron bubble.
Cool it with a baboon's blood,
Then the charm is firm and good.
Macbeth IV i

BEST BRIEF IN COMPETITION

B1.36

O, how that name befits my composition!
Richard II - II i

BILLABLE HOURS - ESCAPING THEM

B1.40

[L]awyers in the vacation: ... they sleep ... and then
they perceive not how time moves.
As You Like It III ii

BILLABLE HOURS - INCREASING THEM

B1.42

Your wit's too hot, it speeds too fast, 'twill tire.
Love's Labour's Lost II i

B1.44
Into what dangers would you lead me, Cassius,
That you would have me seek into myself
For that which is not in me?
Julius Caesar I ii

BILLING
B1.48
Time is the nurse and breeder of all good.
Two Gentlemen of Verona III i

BOILERPLATE IN CONTRACTS
B1.52
[S]icklied o'er with the pale cast of thought
Hamlet III i

Consolidated World v. Finkle, 831 F. 2d 261, 264 (1987). Markey, J.

BRANDEIS BRIEF

B1.64

Glendower: I can call spirits from the vasty deep.

Hotspur: Why, so can I, or so can any man;

But will they come when you do call for them?

1 Henry IV - III i

See also Davis v. State Dept of Corrections, 460 So. 2d 452, 459 (Fla. App. 1984). Joanos, J. A quotation popular with law professors and judges.

BREACH OF PROMISE

B1.68

Dost thou love me? I know thou wilt say "Ay,"

And I will take thy word: yet, if thou swear'st,

Thou mayst prove false; at lovers' perjuries,

They say, Jove laughs.

Romeo and Juliet II ii

BRIEF OF RESPONDENT

B1.72

His reasons are as two grains of wheat hid in two bushels of chaff: you shall seek all day ere you find them, and when you have them, they are not worth the search.

Merchant of Venice I i

BRIEFS

B1.76

Thou has caused printing to be used.

2 Henry VI - IV vii

B1.80

[P]oints more than all the lawyers in Bohemia can learnedly handle.

Winter's Tale IV iv

B1.84
[B]revity is the soul of wit.
Hamlet II ii

See dissent in State v. Eichstedt,
567 A. 2d 1237, 1241 (1989). Spallone, J.

BRIEFS - SECRETARY'S VIEW

B1.88
Here are a few of the unpleasant'st words
That ever blotted paper!
Merchant of Venice III ii

C

CAPIAS
C1.02
Lords, you that here are under our arrest,
Procure your sureties for your days of answer.
Richard II - IV i

CAPITAL PUNISHMENT
C1.08
I have seen,
When, after execution, judgement hath
Repented o'er his doom.
Measure for Measure II ii

C1.12
Put out the light, and then put out the light.
If I quench thee, thou flaming minister,
I can again thy former light restore,
Should I repent me; but once put out thy light,
Thou cunning'st pattern of excelling nature,
I know not where is that Promethean heat
That can thy light relume.
Othello V ii

CASE SYSTEM - STUDENT'S VIEW
C1.20
Bring me no more reports; let them fly all.
Macbeth V iii

CASES - TO TAKE OR NOT TO TAKE
C1.26
A rotten case abides no handling.
2 Henry IV - IV i

CAUSATION

C1.32

What's in a name? ...
That which we call a rose
By any other name would smell as sweet
Romeo & Juliet II ii

Probably the most cited quotation of Shakespeare. Frequently, it is the opening line of the opinion. See Good v. Stevenson, 448 N.Y.S. 2d 981 (1982). Pitaro, J. Cited by Rehnquist, C.J. in Dames & Moore v. Regan, 453 U.S. 654, 675 (1981). Judge Torruella in DiGiovanni v. Traylor Bros., 959 F. 2d 1119, 1124 wrote, "I believe that the counsel found in [this quotation] has definite relevance to the issue that separates my views from those of my colleagues in the majority." And Stone, J. wrote, "An act by any other name would remain the same" in Rapp v. Industrial Commn of Missouri, 360 S.W. 2d 366, 370 (1962). Judge Timbers attempts to define causation, and has to fall back on Shakespeare in Marino v. Otis Eng., 839 F. 2d 1404, 1414 (1988). Also see Conard-Pyle v. Thuren, Inc., 201 U.S.P.Q. 733, 735 (1978): "The plaintiff claims that roses by any other name than 'Star Roses' would not smell as sweet. I have concluded however, that this case is much ado about nothing."

CERTIORARI - DENYING

C1.40

I think, but dare not speak.
Macbeth V i

C1.48

How long a time lies in one little word!
Richard II - I iii

CHARACTER WITNESS
C1.52
For Brutus is an honorable man
Julius Caesar III ii

Cited in dissent by Stevens, J. in Lakeside v.
Oregon, 435 U.S. 333, 346 (1978). See also
State v. Martin, 651 S.W. 2d 645, 656
(1983). Flanigan, J. See also Faramus v. Film
Artistes' Assn. [1963] 2 Q.B. 527.

CHECKS AND BALANCES
C1.60
All must be even in our government.
Richard II - III iv

CIRCUMSTANTIAL EVIDENCE

C1.64

Who finds the heifer dead and bleeding fresh
And sees fast by a butcher with an axe,
But will suspect 'twas he that made the slaughter?
Who finds the partridge in the puttock's nest,
But may imagine how the bird was dead,
Although the kite soar with unbloodied beak?
Even so suspicious is this tragedy.
2 Henry VI - III ii

Wigmore on Evidence, para. 149, p. 584

C1.68

[I]f I shall be condemn'd
Upon surmises, all proofs sleeping else
But what your jealousies awake, I tell you
'Tis rigour and not law.
Winter's Tale III ii

C1.72

Why may not imagination trace the noble dust
of Alexander
Hamlet V i

CITATIONS

C1.76

The devil can cite Scripture for his purpose.
Merchant of Venice I iii

If the devil can, "It is obvious that mere man-made law is likewise
readily available." See In re Eberhardy, 307 N.W. 881, 910 (Wis.)

CIVIL DISOBEDIENCE
C1.80
[W]hen law can do no right,
Let it be lawful that law bar no wrong
King John III i

See Meech v. Hillhaven West, 776 P. 2d 488, 510 (Mont. 1989) for Judge Sheehy's interpretation of this quotation.

CLASS ACTIONS
C1.84
[M]uch throwing about of brains.
Hamlet II ii

CLERKS, JUDICIAL
C1.88
Step aside, and I'll show thee a precedent.
1 Henry IV - II iv

CLIENT TO LAWYER
C1.90
Farewell! thou art too dear for my possessing,
And like enough thou know'st thy estimate.
Sonnet 87

CLIENTS
C1.92
That unlettered small-knowing soul.
Love's Labour's Lost I i

C1.94
[M]inister to a mind diseased.
Macbeth V iii

CLIENTS (CONT.)

C1.96
I'll answer him by law: I'll not budge an inch, boy:
let him come, and kindly.
Taming of the Shrew - Induction i

C2.00
Let me not understand you, then
1 Henry IV - III i

C2.02
[H]e is a stone, a very pebble stone, and has no more
pity in him than a dog
Two Gentlemen of Verona II iii

C2.04
God befriend us, as our cause is just!
1 Henry IV - V i

CLIENTS - AFTER HAVING LAW
EXPLAINED TO THEM
C2.08
What, art thou mad? art thou mad?
is not the truth the truth?
1 Henry IV - II iv

CLIENTS - BANKRUPT
C2.10
[T]he breath of an unfee'd lawyer
King Lear I iv

CLIENTS - EXCUSES
C2.12
This is the excellent foppery of the world, that, when
we are sick in fortune — often the surfeit of our own
behaviour — we make guilty of our disasters the sun,
the moon, and the stars, as if we were villains by
necessity, fools by heavenly compulsion, knaves,
thieves, and treachers, by spherical predominance,
drunkards, liars, and adulterers, by an enforced
obedience of planetary influence, and all that we are
evil in, by a divine thrusting on. An admirable evasion
of whoremaster man, to lay his goatish disposition to
the charge of a star!
King Lear I ii

CLIENTS - FOOLS

C2.16

Puck: Lord, what fools these mortals be!

Midsummer Night's Dream III ii

Vermont v. Schaefer, 599 A. 2d 337, 354 (1992). Dissent by Peck, J. on pretrial publicity.

C2.18

And yet, methinks, I could be well content
To be mine own attorney in this case.

1 Henry VI - V iii

CLIENTS - HEARING THE METER TICKING

C2.24

[E]very minute now
Should be the father of some stratagem

2 Henry IV - I i

CLIENTS - UNWANTED

C2.28

Fortune brings in some boats that are not steer'd.

Cymbeline IV iii

CLIENTS - VIEW OF LAWYERS

C2.30

Dick: The first thing we do, let's kill all the lawyers.
Cade: Nay, that I mean to do. Is not this a lament-
    able thing, that of the skin of an innocent lamb
    should be made parchment? that parchment,
    being scribbled o'er, should undo a man? Some
    say the bee stings: but I say, 'tis the bee's wax;
    for I did but seal once to a thing, and I was
    never mine own man since.

2 Henry VI - IV ii

See Kornstein, Shakespeare and the Law (1994). And for the true context of this quotation, see FIRST STEP TOWARDS AUTOCRACY below.

CLIENTS - VIEW OF LAWYERS (CONT.)

C2.32

To suck, to suck, the very blood to suck!

Henry V - II iii

CLOSING ARGUMENTS

C2.36

Lay on, Macduff, and damn'd be him that first cries
'Hold, enough!'

Macbeth V viii

M. E. Wright v. Dept. of Revenue, 685 P. 2d 418, 425 (1984).
Plaintiff is told to desist in his futile and foolish pleading. Jones, J.

C2.40

If you have tears, prepare to
shed them now.

Julius Caesar III ii

C2.44

There is a history in all men's lives

2 Henry IV - III i

CLOSING ARGUMENTS (CONT.)

C2.48

Friends, Romans, countrymen, — lend me your ears

Julius Caesar III ii

CLOSING ARGUMENTS - POOR

C2.52

[What makes] the unskilful laugh, cannot but make the judicious grieve

Hamlet III ii

See Shaw v. Lindheim, 919 F. 2d 1353, 1360 (1990). Alarcon, J. discusses literary expression and copyright infringement.

COLLECTING FEES

C2.56

All that glisters is not gold

Merchant of Venice II vii

See B. F. Hirsch v. Enright Ref. Co., 617 F. Supp. 49, 51 (1985). Fisher, J.

COLLECTIONS

C2.60

['T]is mine and I will have it.
If you deny me, fie upon your law!
There is no force in the decrees of Venice.
I stand for judgement: answer; shall I have it?

Merchant of Venice IV i

COLOR OF TITLE

C2.64

A deed without a name.

Macbeth IV i

COMITY

C2.68

The Duke cannot deny the course of law:
For the commodity that strangers have
With us in Venice, if it be denied,
Will much impeach the justice of his state;
Since that the trade and profit of the city
Consisteth of all nations.

Merchant of Venice III iii

COMMITMENT FOR PSYCHIATRIC EVALUATION

C2.72

My pulse, as yours, doth temperately keep time,
And makes as healthful music: it is not madness
That I have utter'd; bring me to the test.

Hamlet III iv

Se McCardle v. Tronetti, 769 F. Supp. 188, 189 (1991) for a good explanation of the litigious plaintiff who may not be paranoid.

COMMON AND SEVERAL OWNERSHIPS DISTINGUISHED

C2.76

Boyet: [S]weet lamb, [will] you grant pasture
    for me?
Maid: Not so, gentle beast: my lips are no common,
    though several they be

Love's Labour's Lost II i

COMMUNICATIONS LAW

C2.80

I'll put a girdle round about the earth
In forty minutes.

Midsummer Night's Dream II i

COMMUNITY PROPERTY
C2.84
What's mine is yours, and what is yours is mine.
Measure for Measure V i

CONCURRING OPINIONS
C2.90
Hamlet: Do you see yonder cloud that's almost in
    shape of a camel?
Polonius: By th' mass, and 'tis like a camel indeed.
Hamlet: Methinks it is like a weasel.
Polonius: It is backed like a weasel.
Hamlet: Or like a whale?
Polonius: Very like a whale.
Hamlet III ii

Rex v. Cia. Pervana de Vapores, 660 F. 2d 61, 76 (1981). Sloviter, J.
in dissent. "[T]he judiciary cannot play Polonius to Congress' Hamlet
and so permit legislative lexicography to defeat those rights."

CONFESSIONS
C3.00
No more, but that you read
These accusations and these grievous crimes
Committed by your person and your followers
Against the state and profit of this land;
That, by confessing them, the souls of men
May deem that you are worthily deposed.
Richard II - IV i

CONFLICT OF INTEREST
C3.04
I do perceive here a
divided duty
Othello I iii

CONGRESS, ELECTION TO
C3.08
Hamlet: Ay, marry, why was he sent into England?
Clown: Why, because he was mad; he shall recover
   his wits there; or, if he do not, it's no great
   matter there.
Hamlet: Why?
Clown: 'Twill not be seen in him there; there the
   men are as mad as he.
Hamlet V i

See Yorty v. Chandler, 91 Cal. Rptr. 709, 713 (1971). Fleming, J. has
an excellent analysis of political cartoons, and why mayors should
not bring defamation charges based on them.

CONSCIENCE, GUILTY
C3.12
My conscience hath a thousand several tongues,
And every tongue brings in a several tale,
And every tale condemns me for a villain.
Perjury, perjury, in the highest degree;
All several sins, all used in each degree ...
Throng to the bar crying all, Guilty! Guilty!
Richard III - V iii

CONSIDERATION
C3.16
The cause of this fair gift in me is wanting
Sonnet 87

CONSPIRACY
C3.20
They fell together all, as by consent
The Tempest II i

CONSTITUTIONAL LAW - ORIGINAL INTENT
C3.24
There are more things in heaven and earth, Horatio,
Than are dreamt of in your philosophy.
Hamlet I v

E. C. Curley v. State, 16 So. 2d 440, 443 (Fla. 1944). Brown, J. in dissent.

CONSTITUTIONAL LAWYERS - DREAM
C3.26
[A]nd make new nations.
Henry VIII - V v

CONSTITUTIONAL THEORY

C3.28

More honoured in the breach than the observance.

Hamlet I iv

See U.S. v. Smith, 812 F. 2d 161, 167 (1987). McMillan, J.

CONSTRUCTION OF THE LAW

C3.32

Indeed, it is a strange-disposed time:
But men may construe things after their fashion,
Clean from the purpose of the things themselves.

Julius Caesar I iii

See Tatum v. Schering Corp., 523 So. 2d 1042, 1051 (1988).
Houston, J.

CONTINGENT FEES

C3.36

[Y]our cause of sorrow
Must not be measured by his worth, for then
It hath no end.

Macbeth V viii

C3.40

Ay, there's the rub

Hamlet III i

In re Carthagena Local Sch. Dt., 155 N.E. 2d 267, 272 (1958). Dull, J.

C3.44

The image of it gives me content already; and I trust
it will grow to a most prosperous perfection.

Measure for Measure III i

CONTINUANCES

C3.48

Small things make base men proud

2 Henry VI - IV i

CONTINUING LEGAL EDUCATION
C3.52
Here let us breathe and haply institute
A course of learning and ingenious studies.
Taming of the Shrew I i

CONTRACTS - FORFEITURE CLAUSE
C3.56
Go with me to a notary, seal me there
Your single bond; and, in a merry sport,
If you repay me not on such a day,
In such a place, such sum or sums as are
Express'd in the condition, let the forfeit
Be nominated for an equal pound
Of your fair flesh, to be cut off and taken
In what part of your body pleaseth me.
Merchant of Venice I iii

CONVEYANCING
C3.64
O, what a happy title do I find
Sonnet 92

CORPORATE LAWYER TO HIS CLIENT
C3.70
I shall sutler be
Unto the camp, and profits will accrue.
Give me thy hand.
Henry V - II i

CORPORATE LAWYERS
C3.72
Our hands are full of business
1 Henry IV - III ii

CORPORATE VEIL, PIERCING THE
C3.76
Thy wish was father ... to that thought.
2 Henry IV - IV v

Also see Wright, J. concurring in Rocky River v. Employment Rel. Bd., 530 N.E. 2d 1, 12 (1959): "The most charitable thing I can say concerning the dissent's seemingly prolix treatment of the issues of stare decisis and home rule is the ancient but accurate statement that '[t]hy wish was father ... to that thought.'"

CORRECTING FIRST-YEAR TEST
C3.80
Thou hast the most unsavoury similes
1 Henry IV - I ii

COUNTERCULTURE LAWYER
C3.82
I have neither wit, nor words, nor worth,
Action, nor utterance, nor the power of speech,
To stir men's blood: I only speak right on
Julius Caesar III ii

COUNTRYCULTURE LAWYER
C3.84
I come not, friends, to steal away your hearts:
I am no orator, as Brutus is;
But, as you know me all, a plain blunt man.
Julius Caesar III ii

COURT CALENDAR
C3.88
[']T]is a chronicle of day by day
The Tempest V i

COURT, DAY IN
C3.90
Let Hercules himself do what he may,
The cat will mew and dog will have his day.
Hamlet V i

COURT DECORUM
C3.92
How does thy honour? Let me lick thy shoe.
The Tempest III ii

COURT HOURS
C3.96
Great business must be wrought ere noon.
Macbeth III v

COURT SYSTEM
C4.02
'Tis like the forc'd gait of a shuffling nag.
1 Henry IV - III i

CRAMMING FOR AN EXAM
C4.12
Study is like the heaven's glorious sun,
That will not be deep-search'd
with saucy looks
Love's Labour's Lost I i

CRIME AND PUNISHMENT

C4.20

King Henry: Enlarge the man committed yesterday,
    That rail'd against our person: we consider
    It was excess of wine that set him on;
    And on his more advice we pardon him.
Scroop: That's mercy, but too much security:
    Let him be punish'd, sovereign, lest example
    Breed, by his sufferance, more of such a kind.
King Henry: ... If little faults, proceeding on distemper,
    Shall not be wink'd at, how shall we stretch
        our eye
    When capital crimes, chew'd, swallow'd, and
        digested,
    Appear before us?
Henry V - II ii

CRIMINAL RECORD

C4.24

If thy offences were upon record,
Would it not shame thee in so fair a troop
To read a lecture of them?
Richard II - IV i

Cooke v. Cooke, 319 A. 2d 841, 844 (1974). Lowe, J.

CROSS-EXAMINATION

C4.28

What, will you tear
Impatient answers from my gentle tongue?
Midsummer Night's Dream III ii

C4.32

I am not bound to please thee with my answers.
Merchant of Venice IV i

CROSS-EXAMINATION (CONT.)

C4.36

Urge me no more, I shall forget myself

Julius Caesar IV iii

C4.40

[L]et your reason serve
To make the truth appear where it seems hid,
And hide the false seems true.

Measure for Measure V i

C4.48

Question her proudly; let thy looks be stern:
By this means shall we sound what skill she hath.

1 Henry VI - I ii

CROSS-EXAMINATION OF LAWYER

C4.52

Hamlet: What man dost thou dig it for?

Gravedigger: For no man, sir.

Hamlet: What woman then?

Gravedigger: For none, neither.

Hamlet: Who is to be buried in't?

Gravedigger: One that was a woman, sir; but, rest
    her soul, she's dead.

Hamlet: How absolute the knave is! we must speak
    by the card, or equivocation will undo us.

Hamlet V i

CUSTOM

C4.56

That monster, custom, who all sense doth eat,
Of habits devil, is angel yet in this,
That to the use of actions fair and good
He likewise gives a frock or livery,
That aptly is put on.
Hamlet III iv

D

DEBTORS - UNSECURED

D1.02

I had as lief they would put ratsbane in my mouth
as offer to stop it with security.

2 Henry IV - I ii

DEFAMATION

D1.16

For slander lives upon succession,
For ever hous'd where it once gets possession

Comedy of Errors III i

D1.20

The purest treasure mortal times afford
Is spotless reputation: that away,
Men are but gilded loam or painted clay.
Richard II - I i

D1.24

Good name in man and woman, dear my lord,
Is the immediate jewel of their souls.
Who steals my purse steals trash; 'tis something,
	nothing;
'Twas mine, 'tis his, and has been slave to thousands;
But he that filches from me my good name
Robs me of that which not enriches him
And makes me poor indeed.
Othello III iii

D1.28

What is honour?
A word.
What is in that word, honour? ...
Air. A trim reckoning!
Who hath it?
He that died o' Wednesday.
Doth he feel it?
No.
Doth he hear it?
No.
Is it insensible then?
Yea, to the dead.
But will it not live with the living?
No.
Why?
Detraction will not suffer it.

Therefore, I'll none of it.
Honour is a mere scutcheon:
And so ends my catechism.
1 Henry IV - V i

State ex rel. Cohen v. Manchin, 341 S.E. 2d 852, 853 (W.Va.)
McGraw, J. in dissent. Judge Selya quotes "Honour is a mere
scutcheon" in U.S. v. Dray, 901 F. 2d 1132, 1134 (1990).

D1.30
When you speak best unto the purpose it is not worth
the wagging of your beards; and your beards deserve
not so honourable a grave as to stuff a botcher's
cushion or to be entombed in an ass's packsaddle. Yet
you must be saying, Marcius is proud; who, in a
cheap estimation, is worth all your predecessors since
Deucalion; though peradventure some of the best of
them were hereditary hangmen.
Coriolanus II i

DEFAMATION - BURDEN OF PROOF
D1.32
What answer shall I make to this base man?
Shall I so much dishonour my fair stars,
On equal terms to give him chastisement?
Either I must, or have mine honour soil'd
With the attainder of his slanderous lips. ...
I say, thou liest,
And will maintain what thou hast said is false
Richard II - IV i

DEFENDANT'S RESPONSE TO OPPOSITION WITNESS
D1.34
I say he lies
And lies, and lies
Richard II - IV i

DEFENSE ATTORNEY - SELF-DEFENSE
D1.36
There is some soul of goodness in things evil
Henry V - IV i

DEFENSE ATTORNEY'S VIEW
OF PROSECUTOR
D1.38
A stony adversary, an inhuman wretch
Uncapable of pity, void and empty
From any dram of mercy.
Merchant of Venice IV i

DEFENSE COUNSEL, TEAM OF
D1.40
I think there be six Richmonds in the field.
Richard III - V iv

For the value of this term, see Salazar v. State, 643 S.W. 2d 953, 957 (Texas 1983). Miller, J.

D1.42
With men of courage and with means defendant
Henry V - II iv

DEFENSES, WILD
D1.44
Joan: First, let me tell you whom you have
   condemned ...
  A virgin from her tender infancy,
  Chaste and immaculate in very thought;
  Whose maiden blood, thus rigorously effus'd,
  Will cry for vengeance at the gates of heaven.
York: Ay, ay: — Away with her to execution! ...
Joan: I am with child, ye bloody homicides:
  Murder not, then, the fruit within my womb...

Warwick: The greatest miracle that e'er ye wrought:
    Is all your strict preciseness come to this?
1 Henry VI - V iv

Ligon v. Middtown Area School Dt., 584 A. 2d 376, 379 (Pa. 1990). Smith, J. "Not since Joan DePlucelle ... attempted to defend herself from a capital charge by proclaiming herself a virgin and then, seeing that this particular defense was unlikely to prevail, informed the judge that she was with child, has anyone argued a judicial point with a more breathtaking lack of concern for consistency."

D1.48
I slew him not; but, to mine own disgrace,
Neglected my sworn duty in that case.
Richard II - I i

D1.50
Forbear to judge, for we are sinners all.
2 Henry VI - III iii

DERSHOWITZ, ALAN
D1.52
What impossible matter will he make easy next?
The Tempest II i

DICTATION
D1.54
How use doth breed a habit in man!
Two Gentlemen of Verona V iv

DIGESTS
D1.56
[T]o what end are all these words?
Taming of the Shrew I ii

DISBARMENT

D1.58

Reputation, reputation, reputation! O, I have lost my reputation! I have lost the immortal part of myself, and what remains is bestial.

Othello II iii

D1.60

[C]rack the lawyer's voice,
That he may never more false title plead

Timon of Athens IV iii

DISCOVERY PROCESS

D1.68

Zounds! I was never so bethump'd with words
Since I first call'd my brother's father dad.

King John II i

Hoover v. Barker, 507 S.W. 2d 299, 304 (1974). Shannon, J.

DISSENTING OPINIONS

D1.76

O most lame and impotent conclusion!

Othello II i

D1.82

You speak a language that I understand not.

Winter's Tale III ii

U.S. v. Lynch, 499 F. 2d 1011, 1030. MacKinnon, J. in dissent.

D1.88

Eye of newt and toe of frog,
Wool of bat and tongue of dog.

Macbeth IV i

DISTINGUISHING CASES

D1.92

Comparisons are odorous.

Much Ado About Nothing III v

Conard-Pyle Co. v. Thuron, 201 U.S.P.Q. 733, 735 (1978). Porter, J.

DISTRICT ATTORNEY TO DEFENSE COUNSEL

D1.94

I'll have grounds
More relative than this.

Hamlet II ii

DISTRICT ATTORNEYS

D1.96

[F]ling away ambition.
By that sin fell the angels

Henry VIII - III ii

DISTRICT ATTORNEYS (CONT.)

D1.98
I am coming on,
To venge me as I may and to put forth
My rightful hand in a well-hallow'd cause.
Henry V - I ii

DIVIDED COURT

D2.02
But yet an union in partition
Midsummer Night's Dream III ii

D2.04
And my soul aches
To know, when two authorities are up,
Neither supreme, how soon confusion
May enter 'twixt the gap of both and take
The one by the other.
Coriolanus III i

DIVORCE LAWYER - ADVICE

D2.08
Norfolk: He counsels a divorce; a loss of her
     That, like a jewel, has hung twenty years
     About his neck, yet never lost her lustre;
     Of her that loves him with that excellence
     That angels love good men with; even of her
     That, when the greatest stroke of fortune falls,
     Will bless the King: and is not this course pious?
Lord Chamberlain: Heaven keep me from such
          counsel!
Henry VIII - II ii

DIVORCE LAWYER MEETING THE OTHER SPOUSE
D2.12
[F]oul imaginary eyes of blood
Presented thee more hideous than thou art.
King John IV ii

DOMESTIC RELATIONS
D2.16
Let me not to the marriage of true minds
Admit impediments. Love is not love
Which alters when it alteration finds
Sonnet 116

In re Suzanna, 295 F. 713, 715 (1924). Lowell, J.

DRIVING UNDER THE INFLUENCE
D2.20
Holding the eternal spirit, against her will,
In the vile prison of afflicted breath.
King John III iv

DUE PROCESS
D2.24
What is my offence?
Where are the evidence that do accuse me?
What lawful quest have given their verdict up
Unto the frowning judge? or who pronounced
The bitter sentence of poor Clarence's death?
Before I be convict by course of law,
To threaten me with death is most unlawful.
Richard III - I iv

DUTY TO DISCLOSE

D2.26

[T]ruth will come to light; murder cannot be hid long

Merchant of Venice II ii

Reed v. King, 193 Cal. Rptr. 130 (1983). Blease, J.

DYING DECLARATIONS

D2.28

O, but they say the tongues of dying men
Enforce attention like deep harmony:
Where words are scarce, they are seldom spent
    in vain,
For they breathe truth that breathe their words
    in pain.

Richard II - II i

D2.32

Have I not hideous death within my view...?
What in the world should make me now deceive,
Since I must lose the use of all deceit?
Why should I then be false, since it is true
That I must die here and live hence by truth?

King John V iv

See United Services Auto v. Wharton, 237 F. Supp. 255, 258 (1965).
Craven, J.

E

EAVESDROPPING
E1.02
Unnatural deeds
Do breed unnatural troubles. Infected minds
To their deaf pillows will discharge their secrets.
Macbeth V i

See Com. v. Karmendi, 195 A. 62, 72 (PA 1937). Maxey, J.

ELECTIONS, BAR ASSOCIATION
E1.04
I would with such perfection govern, sir,
To excel the golden age.
The Tempest II i

ENTITLEMENTS

E1.08

[R]epeal daily any wholesome act established against the rich, and provide more piercing statutes daily, to chain up and restrain the poor.

Coriolanus I i

ENVIRONMENTAL LAW

E1.16

[T]his goodly frame, the earth, seems to me a sterile promontory; this most excellent canopy, the air, look you, this brave o'erhanging firmament ... appears no other thing to me than a foul and pestilent congregation of vapours.

Hamlet II ii

Bortz Coal Co. v. Air Pollution Commn. 279 A. 2d 388, 391 (1971). Kramer, J. on air pollution abatement.

EQUITY

E1.20

[C]atch the conscience of the king.

Hamlet II ii

"In sum and in candor, these regulations ... certainly do not 'catch the conscience of the king'" Intl. Union v. Dole, 919 F. 2d 753, 763 (1990). Wald, J. in dissent.

E1.24

Foul subornation is predominant
And equity exiled your Highness' land.

2 Henry VI - III i

E1.28

Thou robed man of justice, take thy place;
And thou, his yoke-fellow of equity,
Bench by his side.

King Lear III vi

E1.32
Falstaff: [T]here's no equity stirring.
1 Henry IV - II ii

Prudence Bonds v. State St. Trust, 202 F. 2d 555, 569 (1953). Frank, J.

E1.36
Oh, she doth teach the torches to burn bright!
It seems she hangs upon the cheek of night
Like a rich jewel in an Ethiope's ear
Romeo & Juliet I v

Nelson v. Nelson, 454 N.W. 2d 533, 538 (S.D. 1990). Henderson, J. talks of "The Lady of Equity is back at our door."

ERA OPPONENTS

E1.38
Frailty, thy name is woman!
Hamlet I ii

This is the opening line in Berni v. Leonard, 331 N.Y.S. 2d 193, 194 (1972). Harnett, J.

ERISA LAWYERS

E1.40
[S]uch a man, so faint, so spiritless,
So dull, so dead in look, so woe begone
2 Henry IV - I i

ESTATE PLANNING

E1.48
Uncertain life, and sure death.
All's Well That Ends Well II iii

E1.52
[M]ust the inheritor himself have no more?
Hamlet V i

EVIDENCE

E1.60

That which you hear, you'll swear you see, there is such unity in the proofs.

Winter's Tale V ii

EVIDENCE - PLANTED

E1.72

Lady Macbeth: Why did you bring these daggers
             from the place?
    They must lie there. Go carry them; and smear
    The sleepy grooms with blood.
Macbeth: I'll go no more...
Lady Macbeth: Give me the daggers...
    I'll gild the faces of the grooms withal;
    For it must seem their guilt.

Macbeth II ii

See Hankins v. Texas, 646 S.W. 2d 191, 203 (Texas 1983). Onion, J. dissenting.

EVIDENCE, TAINTED
E1.76
Out, damned spot!
Macbeth V i

EXECUTORY CONTRACTS
E1.80
[B]ate me some and I will pay you some and, as
most debtors do, promise you infinitely.
2 Henry IV - Epilogue

EXHAUSTION OF REMEDIES
E1.84
[That] is a step
On which I must fall down, or else o'erleap,
For in my way it lies.
Macbeth I iv

Welch v. Gammage, 545 S.W. 2d 223, 226 (1977). Shannon, J.

EXPERT OPINIONS
E1.92
Sermons in stones and good in everything.
As You Like It II i

See Judge Lumbard's dissenting opinion dismissing the opinion of
experts, U.S. v. One Carton, 367 F. 2d 889, 906 (1966).

EXPERT WITNESS
E1.96
I ever have studied physic, through which secret art,
By turning o'er authorities, I have,
Together with my practice, made familiar
To me and to my aid the blest infusions.
Pericles III ii

F

FAIR VALUE
F1.02
A horse! a horse! my kingdom for a horse!
Richard III - V iv

Coca-Cola v. Reeves, 486 S. 2d 374, 392 (1986). Robertson, J. in dissent.

FALSE ACCUSATION
F1.08
Charmian: The man is innocent.
Cleopatra: Some innocents 'scape not the
    thunderbolt.
Antony & Cleopatra II v

FEDERAL BUREAU OF INVESTIGATION
F1.10
[T]he villain shall not 'scape;
The Duke must grant me that. Besides, his picture
I will send far and near, that all the kingdom
May have due note of him
King Lear II i

FEDERAL RULES OF CIVIL PROCEDURE
F1.14
Open, locks,
Whoever knocks!
Macbeth IV i

U.S. v. Arditti, 955 F. 2d 331, 346 (1992). Goldberg, J. concurring.

FEES

F1.16
O'er lawyers' fingers, who straight dream on fees
Romeo & Juliet I iv

FIDUCIARY

F1.18
He hath a wisdom that doth guide his valour
To act in safety.
Macbeth III i

FINES

F1.22
I have an interest in your hate's proceeding,
My blood for your rude brawls doth lie a-bleeding;
But I'll amerce you with so strong a fine
That you shall all repent the loss of mine.
Romeo & Juliet III i

FINES - LIMITATIONS ON USE

F1.26
Dromio: There's no time for a man to recover his
        hair that grows bald by nature.
Antipholus: May he not do it by fine and recovery?
Comedy of Errors II ii

FIRST COURT APPEARANCE

F1.30
The text is old, the orator too green.
Venus and Adonis

FIRST MONDAY IN OCTOBER

F1.32
[W]hat's done is done.
Macbeth III ii

FIRST STEP TOWARDS AUTOCRACY
F1.34
Cade: I thank you, good people: there shall be no
    money; all shall eat and drink on my score; and I
    will apparel them all in one livery, that they may
    agree like brothers and worship me their lord.
Dick Butcher: The first thing we do, let's kill all the
    lawyers.
2 Henry VI - IV ii

FOLLOWING ORDERS
F1.36
[I]f his cause be wrong, our obedience to the King
wipes the crime of it out of us.
Henry V - IV i

F1.38
Every subject's duty is the King's; but every subject's
soul is his own.
Henry V - IV i

FOOTNOTES

F1.46
Small have continual plodders ever won
Save base authority from others' books.
Love's Labour's Lost I i

FORNICATION, LAWS AGAINST

F1.52
The law hath not been dead, though it hath slept.
Measure for Measure II ii

The opening line of Judge Wisdom's opinion in Labat v. Bennett, 365 F. 2d 698, 701 (1966).

FRAUD

F1.54
The man that once did sell the lion's skin
While the beast liv'd was kill'd with hunting him.
Henry V - IV iii

FREE SPEECH

F1.56
[G]iving reins and spurs to my free speech
Richard II - I i

F1.60
[I]mpartial are our eyes and ears:
Were he my brother, nay, my kingdom's heir ...
Now, by my sceptre's awe, I make a vow ...
He is our subject,;Mowbray, so art thou:
Free speech and fearless I to thee allow.
Richard II - I i

F1.64
I do arrest your words.
Measure for Measure II iv

FREE SPEECH (CONT.)
F1.66
And art made tongue-tied by authority
Sonnet 66

FREEDOM OF INFORMATION ACT
F1.70
Masking the business from the common eye
For sundry weighty reasons.
Macbeth III i

G

GRAND JURY
G1.02
Something [was] rotten in the state of Denmark.
Hamlet I iv

"Literary references, like hyperbole, are a part of our legal heritage and language..." Texas Health v. Krell, 828 S.W. 2d 192, 204 (1992). Bissett, J.

G1.04
You are grand-jurors, are ye? we'll jure ye, 'faith.
1 Henry IV - II ii

GREAT CASES MAKING BAD LAW
G1.08
[T]hat superfluous case
That hid the worse and show'd the better face.
Love's Labour's Lost V ii

GUILT
G1.12
Suspicion always haunts the guilty mind;
The thief doth fear each bush an officer.
3 Henry VI - V vi

G1.16
What, will these hands ne'er be clean?
Macbeth V i

GUILTY DEFENDANT

G1.20

My lord, we have
Stood here observing him. Some strange commotion
Is in his brain; he bites his lip, and starts;
Stops on a sudden, looks upon the ground,
Then lays his finger on his temple; straight
Springs out into fast gait; then stops again,
Strikes his breast hard, and anon he casts
His eye against the moon. In most strange postures
We have seen him set himself.
Henry VIII - III ii

GUILTY VERDICTS

G1.24

Sad tidings bring I to you.
1 Henry VI - I i

H

HAIR-SPLITTING

H1.02

I'll cavil on the ninth part of a hair.

1 Henry IV - III i

See U.S. v. Jones, 176 F. 2d 278, 290 (1949). Yankwich, J.

HEARSAY RULE

H1.12

Rumour is a pipe
Blown by surmises, jealousies, conjectures,
And of so easy and so plain a stop
That the blunt monster with uncounted heads,
The still-discordant wavering multitude,
Can play upon it ... from Rumour's tongues
They bring smooth comforts false, worse than
    true wrongs.

2 Henry IV - Induction

HIRING COMMITTEE

H1.20

Will you tell me, Master Shallow, how to choose a
man? Care I for the limb, the thewes, the stature,
bulk, and big assemblance of a man! Give me the
spirit, Master Shallow.

2 Henry IV - III ii

HORNBOOKS - NIGHTMARE AFTER
READING TOO MANY

H1.22

O God, I could be bounded in a nutshell

Hamlet II ii

HOSTILE WITNESSES –
ON TURNING STATE'S EVIDENCE
H1.24
Ye have angels' faces,
but heaven knows your hearts.
Henry VIII - III i

HOUSE COUNSEL
H1.28
[A]nd bestow
Your needful counsel to our business,
Which craves the instant use.
King Lear II i

HYPOTHETICAL CASES
H1.32
Present fears
Are [often] less than horrible imaginings.
Macbeth I iii

In re Pearson, 990 F. 2d 653, 661 (1993), Selya, J. In Ernst & Young
v. Depositors Economic Protection Corps, 45 F. 3d 530, 538 (1995).

I

ILLEGITIMACY

I1.02

Legitimate Edgar, I must have your land:
Our father's love is to the bastard Edmund.
As to the legitimate: fine word, legitimate!
Well, my legitimate, if this letter speed,
And my invention thrive, Edmund the base
Shall top the legitimate. I grow; I prosper.—
Now, gods, stand up for bastards!
King Lear I ii

I1.04

Sirrah, your brother is legitimate;
Your father's wife did after wedlock bear him,
And if she did play false, the fault was hers;
Which fault lies on the hazards of all husbands
That marry wives. Tell me, how if my brother,
Who, as you say, took pains to get this son,
Had of your father claim'd this son for his?
In sooth, good friend, your father might have kept
This calf bred from his cow from all the world;
In sooth he might; then, if he were my brother's,
My brother might not claim him; nor your father,
Being none of his, refuse him: this concludes;
My mother's son did get your father's heir;
Your father's heir must have your father's land.
King John I i

See R.R.K. v. S.G.P., 507 N.E. 2d 736, 739 (Mass. 1987). Liacos, J.

IMMUNITY
I1.08
Thou canst not say I did it.
Macbeth III iv

IN CAMERA HEARING
I1.12
Then call them to our presence; face to face,
And frowning brow to brow, ourselves will hear
The accuser and the accused freely speak
Richard II - I i

See Coy v. Iowa, 487 U.S. 1012, 1016 (1988). Scalia, J. See also
Blackmun's dissent at p. 1029. See also 5 Wigmore, Evid. para.
1395, p. 153 n. 2 (J. Chadbourn rev. 1974)

INJUSTICE
I1.16
Thrice is he arm'd that hath his quarrel just,
And he but naked, though lock'd up in steel,
Whose conscience with injustice is corrupted.
2 Henry VI - III ii

INNOCENCE - ONE'S OWN
I1.20
[A]s clear as is the summer's sun
Henry V - I ii

INSANITY - DURHAM RULE
I1.24
Diseased Nature oftentimes breaks forth
In strange eruptions.
1 Henry IV - III i

INSANITY DEFENSE
I1.28
[F]or, to define true madness,
What is't but to be
nothing else but mad?
Hamlet II ii

I1.32
Though this be madness, yet there is method in't.
Hamlet II ii

INTENT
I1.36
My brother had but justice,
In that he did the thing for which he died.
For Angelo,
His act did not o'ertake his bad intent,
And must be buried but as an intent
That perish'd by the way. Thoughts are no subjects,
Intents but merely thoughts.
Measure for Measure V i

See Rehnquist, C.J. in U.S. v. Apfelbaum, 445 U.S. 115, 131 (1980)
and his discussion of "anticipatory perjury."

INTERNAL REVENUE CODE
I1.44
Was ever book containing such vile matter
So fairly bound?
Romeo & Juliet III ii

INTERNATIONAL LAW - VIOLATION OF
I1.48
Uproar the universal peace, confound
All unity on earth.
Macbeth IV iii

INTERROGATORIES
I1.52
And charge us there upon inter'gatories,
And we will answer all things faithfully.
Merchant of Venice V i

J

JAILHOUSE LAWYERS
J1.02
And on the winking of authority
To understand a law
King John IV ii

JUDGE
J1.04
All men's honours
Lie like one lump before him, to be fashion'd
Into what pitch he please.
Henry VIII - II ii

JUDGE - IRASCIBLE
J1.06
How tartly that gentleman looks! I never can see him
but I am heart-burned an hour after.
Much Ado About Nothing II i

JUDGE - OVERRULED
J1.08
Beat at this gate, that let thy folly in,
    [*striking his head*]
And thy dear judgment out!
King Lear I iv

JUDGE TO COUNSEL
J1.10
My lord, methinks, is very long in talk.
1 Henry VI - I ii

JUDGE TO COUNSEL (CONT.)

J1.12

Duke: You were not bid to speak.

Lucio: No, my good lord:
   Nor wish'd to hold my peace.

Duke: I wish you now, then;
   Pray you, take note of it: and when you have
   A business for yourself, pray Heaven you then
   Be perfect

Measure for Measure V i

JUDGE - TRYING TO UNDERSTAND COUNSEL'S OBJECTION

J1.14

Once more unto the breach, dear friend, once more

Henry V - III i

"But ... cases cited by the plaintiff, fairly read, cannot carry the weight which she assigns them." Selya, J. in Hartman v. Providence, 636 F. Supp. 1395, 1412 (1986).

JUDGE'S CREDO

J1.16

This above all: to thine own self be true,
And it must follow, as the night the day,
Thou canst not then be false to any man.

Hamlet I iii

This is the credo of Klein, J. in South Euclid v. Bondy, 200 N.E. 2d 508, 512 (Ohio 1964).

JUDGES

J1.22

Some are born great, some achieve greatness, and some have greatness thrust upon 'em.

Twelfth Night II v

J1.24
[A] thing ensky'd and sainted
Measure for Measure I iv

J1.26
Free from gross passion or of mirth or anger,
Constant in spirit, not swerving with the blood,
Garnish'd and deck'd in modest complement,
Not working with the eye without the ear,
And but in purged judgement trusting neither
Henry V - II ii

J1.28
May he ... do justice
For truth's sake and his conscience; that his bones,
When he has run his course and sleeps in blessings,
May have a tomb of orphans' tears wept on 'em!
Henry VIII - III ii

JUDGES (CONT.)

J1.36

The prince of darkness is a gentleman.
King Lear III iv

J1.40

O, it is excellent
To have a giant's strength: but it is tyrannous
To use it like a giant.
Measure for Measure II ii

J1.42

[M]en's judgements are
A parcel of their fortunes, and things outward
Do draw the inward quality after them,
To suffer all alike.
Antony & Cleopatra III xiii

JUDGES - AS SEEN BY THE PUBLIC

J1.44

Holland: [A]nd yet it is said, "Labour in thy
        vocation;" which is as much to say as, "Let
        the magistrates be labouring men; and therefore
        should we be magistrates."
Bevis: Thou hast hit it; for there's no better sign of a
        brave mind than a hard hand.
2 Henry VI - IV ii

JUDGES - ATTITUDE

J1.46

More authority, dear boy, name more
Love's Labour's Lost I ii

J1.48

[L]et me take you a button-hole lower.
Love's Labour's Lost V ii

JUDGES - ATTITUDE (CONT.)

J1.50

Chief Justice: [W]hat I did, I did in honour,
Led by the impartial conduct of my soul
2 Henry IV - V ii

J1.52

[T]he things I speak are just.
2 Henry IV - V iii

JUDGES - BAD EXAMPLES

J1.56

[T]hey by observing of him, do bear themselves like
foolish justices
2 Henry IV - V i

J1.58

Thieves for their robbery have authority
When judges steal themselves.
Measure for Measure II ii

JUDGES - CITING SHAKESPEARE

J1.66

No ceremony that to great ones 'longs,
Not the king's crown, not the deputed sword,
The Marshal's truncheon, nor the judge's robe
Becomes them with one half so good a grace
Measure for Measure II ii

JUDGES - DISSENTING OPINON

J1.74

Clown: What thinkest thou of his opinion?
Malvolio: I think nobly of the soul, and no way
     approve his opinion.
Twelfth Night IV ii

JUDGES - FAIR AND IMPARTIAL

J1.82

O wise young judge, how I do honour thee!

Merchant of Venice IV i

See People v. De Jesus, 369 N.E. 2d 752, 755 (N.Y. 1977), where
Cooke, J. considered a case of judicial misconduct.

JUDGES - HONORABLE

J1.90

Justice with favour have I always done;
Prayers and tears have moved me, gifts could never.

2 Henry VI - IV vi

JUDGES - INFLUENCING

J1.96

[A] friend i' the court is better than a penny in purse.

2 Henry IV - V i

JUDGES - INSTRUCTIONS TO JURY

J1.98

The sad-eyed justice, with his surly hum,
Delivering o'er to executors pale
The lazy yawning drone.

Henry V - I ii

JUDGES - LEGISLATING

J2.00

Wrest once the law to your authority:
To do a great right, do a little wrong

Merchant of Venice IV i

Rand v. State, 341 S.W. 2d 9, 13 (Ark. 1960). McFaddin concurring.

JUDGES - OPINION OF PUBLIC INTEREST LAWYERS
J2.04
Chief Justice: I am well acquainted with your manner of wrenching the true cause the false way.
2 Henry IV - II i

JUDGES - OUTBURSTS
J2.06
This inundation of mistemper'd humour
King John V i

JUDGES' PHOBIA
J2.08
Chief Justice: O God, I fear all will be overturn'd.
2 Henry IV - V ii

JUDGES - QUALIFICATIONS
J2.12
[A] gentleman of excellent breeding, admirable discourse, of great admittance, authentic in your place and person, generally allowed for your many war-like, court-like, and learned preparations.
Merry Wives of Windsor II ii

J2.16
Dogberry: I am a wise fellow, and, which is more, an officer, and, which is more, a householder, and, which is more, as pretty a piece of flesh as any is in Messina, and one that knows the law.
Much Ado About Nothing IV ii

JUDGES - SIDEBAR CONFERENCE
J2.22
A plague o' both your houses.
Romeo & Juliet III i

J. F. Edwards v. Anderson Safeway, 542 F. 2d 1318, 1324 (1976).

JUDGES - STATESMANSHIP
J2.24
To cast beyond ourselves in our opinions
Hamlet II i

JUDGES - TURNING THE COURT OVER TO LAWYERS
J2.26
When thou gavest them the rod, and puttest down thine own breeches,
>   *Then they for sudden joy did weep,*
>   *And I for sorrow sung,*
>   *That such a king should play bo-peep,*
>   *And go the fools among*
King Lear I iv

JUDGES, YOUNG
J2.28
My salad days,
When I was green in judgement
Antony & Cleopatra I v

JUDGMENT, REVERSAL OF
J2.30
O judgement! thou art fled to brutish beasts,
And men have lost their reason.
Julius Caesar III ii

Owens v. Whitwell, 481 So. 2d 1071, 1077 (Mississippi 1986). Lee, J.

JUDICIAL CLICHES
J2.32
[T]he justice, ...
Full of wise saws and modern instances
As You Like It II vii

JUDICIAL PURISTS
J2.36
Interpretation will misquote our looks
1 Henry IV - V ii

JURIES
J2.40
[There] have been grand-jurymen since before Noah
was a sailor.
Twelfth Night III ii

See Huebner v. Dt. Ct., 490 A. 2d 266, 268 (Md. 1985). Gilbert, J.

J2.44

The jury, passing on the prisoner's life,
May in the sworn twelve have a thief or two
Guiltier than him they try.
Measure for Measure II i

See Florida v. Serra, 529 So. 2d 1262, 1263 (Fla. 1988). Per curiam.

J2.48

[E]yes are open ... but their sense is shut.
Macbeth V i

See: Colorado v. Connelly, 479 U.S. 157, 172 (1986). Stevens, J.
Used in the sense of involuntary reactions as relating to evidence.

JURIES - ENNUI

J2.52

[T]wice-told tale
King John III iv

U.S. v. Arboleda, 20 F. 3d 58, 62 (1994). Cardamone, J.

JURISDICTION
J2.56
Ripeness is all.
King Lear V ii

JURISPRUDENCE
J2.60
Adversity's sweet milk, philosophy
Romeo & Juliet III iii

JUST WARS
J2.64
[T]he arms are fair,
When the intent of bearing them is just.
1 Henry IV - V ii

JUSTICE
J2.68
[T]he baseless fabric of this vision ... this
insubstantial pageant.
The Tempest IV i

J2.70
Speed: If you love her, you cannot see her.
Valentine: Why?
Speed: Because Love is blind.
Two Gentlemen of Verona II i

J2.72
She's beautiful and therefore to be woo'd;
She is a woman, therefore to be won.
1 Henry VI - V iii

JUSTICE (CONT.)

J2.76

May one be pardon'd and retain the offence?
In the corrupted currents of this world
Offence's gilded hand may shove by justice,
And oft 'tis seen the wicked prize itself
Buys out the law: But 'tis not so above;
There is no shuffling, there the action lies
In his true nature; and we ourselves compell'd,
Even to the teeth and forehead of our faults,
To give in evidence.
Hamlet III iii

J2.80

You are right, Justice, and you weigh this well;
Therefore still bear the balance and the sword:
And I do wish your honours may increase,
Till you do live to see a son of mine
Offend you and obey you, as I did.
So shall I live to speak my father's words:
"Happy am I, that have a man so bold,
That dares do justice on my proper son;
And not less happy, having such a son,
That would deliver up his greatness so
Into the hands of Justice." You did commit me:
For which, I do commit into your hand
The unstained sword that you have used to bear;
With this remembrance, that you use the same
With the like bold, just and impartial spirit
As you have done 'gainst me. There is my hand.
2 Henry IV - V ii

JUSTICE (CONT.)

J2.82

[A]s thou urgest justice, be assur'd
Thou shalt have justice, more than thou desir'st.
Merchant of Venice IV i

JUSTICE - IN THE BALANCE

J2.84

Take but degree away, untune that string,
And, hark, what discord follows!
Force should be right; or rather, right and wrong,
Between whose endless jar justice resides,
Should lose their names, and so should justice too.
Then everything includes itself in power,
Power into will, will into appetite;
And appetite, an universal wolf, ...
Must make perforce an universal prey,
And last eat up himself.
Troilus & Cressida I iii

See Bredvold, The Meaning of the Concept of Right Reason in the
Natural Law Tradition, 36 Univ. of Detroit Law Jl. 124 (1958-59).

JUSTICE - INEQUALITY OF

J2.88

Lear: A man may see how this world goes with no
      eyes. Look with thine ears: see how yon justice
      rails upon yon simple thief. Hark, in thine ear:
      change places; and, handy-dandy, which is the
      justice, which is the thief? Thou hast seen a
      farmer's dog bark at a beggar?
Gloucester: Ay, sir.
Lear: And the creature run from the cur? There thou
      mightst behold the great image of authority: a
      dog's obeyed in office. — Thou rascal beadle,
      hold thy bloody hand!

Why doest thou lash that whore? Strip thine own
    back;
Thou hotly lust'st to use her in that kind
For which thou whipp'st her. The usurer hangs the
    cozener.
Through tatter'd clothes small vices do appear;
Robes and furr'd gowns hide all. Plate sin with gold,
And the strong lance of justice hurtless breaks;
Arm it in rags, a pigmy's straw does pierce it.
None does offend, none, I say, none; I'll able 'em
Take that of me, my friend, who have the power
To seal the accuser's lips. Get thee glass eyes;
And, like a scurvy politician, seem
To see the things thou dost not. Now, now, now, now.
King Lear IV vi

JUSTICE, LIMITATIONS OF
J2.94
[I]n the course of justice, none of us
Should see salvation
Merchant of Venice IV i

L

LATE FILING
L1.02
When remedies are past, the griefs are ended
By seeing the worst, which late on hopes depended.
To mourn a mischief that is past and gone
Is the next way to draw new mischief on.
Othello I iii

LAW
L1.04
I stand here for law.
Merchant of Venice IV i

L1.08
[O]ld father antic the law
1 Henry IV - I ii

L1.12
The vasty fields.
Henry V - Prologue

L1.18
[I]t was Greek to me.
Julius Caesar I ii
Bruner v. League Genl. Ins. Co., 416 N.W. 2d 318, 319

LAW FACULTY
L1.20
We few, we happy few, we band of brothers
Henry V - IV iii

LAW FIRM, THE

L1.22
All the world's a stage,
And all the men and women merely players:
They have their exits and their entrances;
And one man in his time plays many parts
As You Like It II vii

LAW FIRM - DOWNSIZING

L1.24
This was the most unkindest cut of all
Julius Caesar III ii

LAW FIRM - SETTING UP

L1.32
I would to God thou and I knew where a commodity
of good names were to be bought.
1 Henry IV - I ii

LAW FIRMS, DEAD PARTNERS IN TITLES OF

L1.36
[T]hou art mighty yet!
Thy spirit walks abroad.
Julius Caesar V iii

L1.38
[O]ur names
Familiar in his mouth as household words.
Henry V - IV iii

LAW FIRMS - THE 80s

L1.40

[G]reat weeds do grow apace.

Richard III - II iv

See Sisk v. Williamson County, 632 N.E. 2d 672, 680 (Ill. 1994). Lewis, J. in dissent on the duty of care.

LAW LIBRARIAN

L1.42

[*Takes a skull*] Alas, poor Yorick! I knew him, Horatio; a fellow of infinite jest, of most excellent fancy: he hath borne me on his back a thousand times; and now, how abhorred in my imagination it is! my gorge rises at it. ... Where be your gibes now? your gambols? your songs? your flashes of merriment, that were wont to set the table on a roar?

Hamlet V i

LAW OFFICES

L1.44

Why so large cost, having so short a lease, Dost thou upon thy fading mansion spend?

Sonnet 146

LAW PROFESSOR

L1.48

[W]hen I am forgotten, as I shall be ...
[S]ay, I taught thee

Henry VIII - III ii

L1.52
Turn him to any cause of policy,
The Gordian knot of it he will unloose,
Familiar as his garter:—that, when he speaks,
The air, a charter'd libertine, is still,
And the mute wonder lurketh in men's ears,
To steal his sweet and honey'd sentences
Henry V - I i

L1.56
This just and learned priest
Henry VIII - II ii

LAW PROFESSOR (CONT.)

L1.60
He was a scholar, and a ripe and good one
Henry VIII - IV ii

L1.64
[E]xceedingly fantastical: too too vain, too too vain.
Love's Labour's Lost V ii

L1.68
There will little learning die ... that day thou
art hanged.
Timon of Athens II ii

L1.72
Such a nature,
Tickled with good success, disdains the shadow
Which he treads at noon
Coriolanus I ii

LAW PROFESSOR - FIRST WORDS
OF SEMESTER

L1.76
And thou shalt see how apt it is to learn
Any hard lesson that may do thee good.
Much Ado About Nothing I i

LAW PROFESSOR - TENURE

L1.78
And future ages groan for this foul act
Richard II - IV i

LAW PROFESSOR - WARNING
L1.80
[B]e you silent and attentive too,
For he that interrupts [me] shall not live.
3 Henry VI - I i

LAW REVIEW ARTICLES
L1.82
Polonius: What do you read, my lord?
Hamlet: Words, words, words
Hamlet II ii

In State v. Schaefer, 599 A. 2d 337, 349 (Vt. 1992), Peck, J. uses the words of Hamlet to characterize the majority opinion. Cited with approval by Judge Urbigkit in Duffy v. State, 837 P. 2d 1047, 1054 (Wyo. 1992), also in dissent.

LAW REVIEW NOTE WRITER
L1.84
I will have that subject newly writ o'er, that I may example my digression by some mighty precedent.
Love's Labour's Lost I ii

LAW REVIEW, SUBMITTING ARTICLE TO
L1.88
When thou reviewest this, thou dost review
The very part was consecrate to thee
Sonnet 74

LAW REVUES
L1.92
[L]aughter for a month and good jest for ever.
1 Henry IV - II ii

LAW SCHOOL ALUMNI - MEMORIES
L1.94
Justice Shallow:
Jesu, Jesu, the mad days
that I have spent!
2 Henry IV - III ii

LAW SCHOOL DEAN
L1.96
O, my offence is rank
Hamlet III iii

LAW SCHOOL GRADUATION
L2.00
Caesar, I never stood on ceremonies,
Yet now they fright me ...
Horses did neigh, and dying men did groan,
And ghosts did shriek and squeal about the streets.

O Caesar! these things are beyond all use,
And I do fear them.
Julius Caesar II ii

See Ideal Mutual Ins. Co. v. Last Days Evan. Assn., 783 F. 2d 1234, 1235 (1986). Goldberg, J.

L2.04
O Ceremony, show me but thy worth! ...
Art thou aught else but place, degree, and form,
Creating awe and fear in other men?
Henry V - IV i

LAW STUDENT - CALLED ON

L2.12
I am so vexed, that every part
about me quivers.
Romeo & Juliet II iv

L2.16
[P]ardon me,
That I have given no answer all this while
2 Henry VI - V i

L2.20
Why do you look on us, and shake your head?
Richard III - II ii

L2.26
What, will you tear
Impatient answers from my gentle tongue?
Midsummer Night's Dream III ii

LAW STUDENT - DREAMS
L2.34
O, had I but followed the arts!
Twelfth Night I iii

LAW STUDENT - FIRST YEAR
L2.36
Biron: I have already sworn ...
    [T]o live and study here three years. ...
    O, these are barren tasks, too hard to keep, ...
    What is the end of study? let me know.
King: Why, that to know, which else we should
    not know.
Biron: Things hid and barr'd, you mean, from
    common sense?
King: Ay, that is study's godlike recompense.
Love's Labour's Lost I i

L2.38
Put not yourself into amazement how these things
should be. All difficulties are but easy when they
are known.
Measure for Measure IV ii

LAW STUDENT - FLUNKING
L2.40
Ye turn me into nothing. Woe upon ye
And all such false professors!
Henry VIII - III i

LAW STUDENT - GOOD GRADES WITHOUT STUDYING
L2.44
[H]is addiction was to courses vain,
His companies unletter'd, rude, and shallow,
His hours fill'd up with riots, banquets, sports,
And never noted in him any study,
Any retirement, any sequestration
From open haunts and popularity.
Henry V - I i

LAW STUDENT - LAW REVIEW REJECT
L2.48
I am not ... lean enough to be thought a good
student
Twelfth Night IV ii

LAW STUDENT - REMINDER TO SELF
L2.52
[I]t shall do you no harm to learn.
All's Well that Ends Well II ii

LAW STUDENT TO LAW PROFESSOR
L2.58
You cram these words into mine ears against
The stomach of my sense.
The Tempest II i

LAW STUDENT WHO CHOSE
LAW OVER MEDICINE
L2.60
Throw physic to the dogs; I'll none of it.
Macbeth V iii

L2.62
Thus have I shunn'd the fire, for fear of burning,
And drench'd me in the sea, where I am drown'd
Two Gentlemen of Verona I iii

LAW STUDENTS - DURING EXAM
L2.64
[I]t never yet did hurt
To lay down likelihoods
2 Henry IV - I iii

LAW STUDENTS - GRADUATION
L2.66
That you do bend your eye on vacancy
Hamlet III iv

LAW STUDENTS - OPINION OF EXAM QUESTIONS
L2.70
[T]he text is foolish.
King Lear IV ii

LAWMAKERS
L2.74
I will make it felony to drink small beer.
2 Henry VI - IV ii

LAWYER AS PROPHET
L2.76
Take note, take note, O world,
To be direct and honest is not safe.
Othello III iii

LAWYER-CLIENT PRIVILEGE
L2.78
The players cannot keep counsel. They'll tell all.
Hamlet III ii

LAWYER - ON HIGHEST HORSE
L2.80
How high a pitch his resolution soars!
Richard II - I i

LAWYER - POST-ETHICS INVESTIGATION
L2.82
Not a hair perish'd;
On their sustaining garments not a blemish,
But fresher than before
The Tempest I ii

LAWYER WHO DOESN'T GET IT
L2.84
Malcolm: Dispute it like a man.
Macbeth: I shall do so;
    But I must also feel it as a man.
Macbeth IV iii

LAWYER WRITING A BRIEF
L2.86
I have
Immortal longings in me.
Antony & Cleopatra V ii

LAWYER'S ATTITUDE
L2.88
Come what come may,
Time and the hour runs through
    the roughest day.
Macbeth I iii

LAWYERS

L2.90

What a piece of work is [a lawyer]!
How noble in reason! How infinite in faculty!
In form, in moving, how express and admirable!
In action how like an angel!
In apprehension how like a god!

Hamlet II ii

See City of St. Louis v. Klocker, 637 S.W. 2d 174, 179
(Missouri 1982). Judge Pudlowski justifies his dissent
and his support of the law of necessity with this quote.

L2.92

[G]ood counselors lack no clients.
Measure for Measure I ii

LAWYERS (CONT.)

L2.96

Advocate's the court-word for a pheasant.
Winter's Tale IV iv

L3.00

[T]he cankers of a calm world and a long peace
1 Henry IV - IV ii

L3.02

[I]t oft falls out,
To have what we would have, we speak not
what we mean.
Measure for Measure II iv

LAWYERS - ABILITY TO LISTEN TO CLIENTS

L3.06

Tying thine ear to no tongue but thine own!
1 Henry IV - I iii

LAWYERS - BREACH OF FIDUCIARY DUTY

L3.10

Oft expectation fails, and most oft there
Where most it promises
All's Well That Ends Well II i

LAWYERS - DEAD

L3.12

Why may not that be the skull of a lawyer? Where be
his quiddities now, his quillets, his cases, his tenures,
and his tricks? Why does he suffer this rude knave
now to knock him about the sconce with a dirty
shovel, and will not tell him of his action of battery?
Hum! This fellow might be in's time a great buyer of
land, with his statutes, his recognizances, his fines, his

double vouchers, his recoveries. Is this the fine of his fines, and the recovery of his recoveries, to have his fine pate full of fine dirt? Will his vouchers vouch him no more of his purchases, and double ones too, than the length and breadth of a pair of indentures? The very conveyances of his lands will hardly lie in this box; and must the inheritor himself have no more, ha?
Hamlet V i

Cited in a case of an attorney who would not pay his bar association dues. In re R. I. Bar Assn., 374 A. 2d 802, 804 (R.I. 1977). Kelleher, J.

LAWYERS DO IT
L3.14

Justice Shallow: I was once of Clement's Inn, where I think they will talk of mad Shallow yet.

Silence: You were called lusty Shallow then, cousin.

Shallow: By the mass, I was called any thing; and I would have done any thing indeed, too, and roundly too. There was I, and little John Doit of Staffordshire, and black George Barnes, and Francis Pickbone, and Will Squele, a Cotswold man;— you had not four such swinge-bucklers in all the inns o' Court again: and I may say to you, we knew where the bona-robas [literally, "good dresses"] were and had the best of them all at commandment.
2 Henry IV - III ii

LAWYERS - ELECTION TO BAR ASSOCIATION COMMITTEES
L3.16

[F]or who shall go about
To cozen fortune, and be honourable
Without the stamp of merit?
Merchant of Venice II ix

LAWYERS - FEELING SORRY FOR THEMSELVES

L3.18

So shaken as we are, so wan with care
1 Henry IV - I i

LAWYERS, IN DEFENSE OF

L3.20

If you prick us, do we not bleed?
if you tickle us, do we not laugh?
if you poison us, do we not die?
Merchant of Venice III i

LAWYERS - JOYS

L3.22

[A]nd it is great
To do that thing that ends all other deeds;
Which shackles accidents and bolts up change
Antony & Cleopatra V ii

LAWYERS - KNOWLEDGE OF THE LAW
L3.26
Faith, I have been a truant in the law,
And never yet could frame my will to it;
And therefore frame the law unto my will ...
I have perhaps some shallow spirit of judgment;
But in these nice sharp quillets of the law,
Good faith, I am no wiser than a daw.
1 Henry VI - II iv

Cited by Judge Gewin in Labat v. Bennett, 365 F. 2d 698, 729 (1966), with reference to habeas corpus

LAWYERS - SAYING GOODNIGHT
L3.30
A thousand times good night!
Romeo & Juliet II ii

LAWYERS - WASHINGTON
L3.34
Costly thy habit as thy purse can buy,
But not express'd in fancy; rich, not gaudy!
For the apparel oft proclaims the man.
Hamlet I iii

LAWYERS - WHEN TOO PROSAIC
L3.40
The man that hath no music in himself,
Nor is not moved with concord of sweet sounds,
Is fit for treasons, strategems and spoils;
The motions of his spirit are dull as night
And his affections dark as Erebus:
Let no such man be trusted. Mark the music.
Merchant of Venice V i

See People v. Ziegler, 214 N.Y.S. 2d 177, 185 (1961). Bayer, J. saves the day for chamber music.

LAWYERS WHO ENVY JOHN GRISHAM
L3.46
I had rather than forty shillings I had my Book of
Songs and Sonnets here.
Merry Wives of Windsor I i

LEGAL AID
L3.52
'Tis not enough to help the feeble up
Timon of Athens I i

LEGAL CAREER
L3.60
And so, from hour to hour, we ripe and ripe,
And then, from hour to hour, we rot and rot
As You Like It II vii

LEGAL FICTION
L3.66
[F]alse shadows for true substances.
Titus Andronicus III ii

LEGAL LOOPHOLES
L3.70
We must not make a scarecrow of the law,
Setting it up to fear the birds of prey,
And let it keep one shape, till custom make it
Their perch and not their terror.
Measure for Measure II i

Collazo v. Estelle, 940 F. 2d 411, 433 (1991), dissent by O'Scannlain, J.
J. Rothwax, author of *Guilty: The Collapse of Criminal Justice*
(1996), would approve of this opinion.

LEGAL PRACTICE TODAY
L3.72
We have seen better days.
Timon of Athens IV ii

L3.74
Now is the winter of our discontent
Richard III - I i

LEGAL PUBLISHER
L3.76
I will never fail
Beginning nor supplyment.
Cymbeline III iv

LEGAL RESEARCH
L3.78
By indirections find directions out.
Hamlet II i

LEGAL SECRETARY
L3.80
I am constant as the northern star.
Julius Caesar III i

LEGISLATIVE PROCESS
L3.84
Dick: [T]hat the laws of England may come out of
     your mouth.
Holland: [*aside*] Mass, 'twill be sore law, then...
Smith: [*aside*] Nay, John, it will be stinking law; for
     his breath stinks with eating toasted cheese.
Cade: ... [B]urn all the records of the realm: my
     mouth shall be the parliament of England.

Holland: [*aside*] Then we are like to have biting
statutes, unless his teeth be pulled out.
2 Henry VI - IV vii

LITIGATION -
DECISION TO SUE
L3.90
Cry 'Havoc,' and let slip
the dogs of war
Julius Caesar III i

See Fiscal Court v. Louisville, 559 S.W.
2d 478, 481 (1977). Jones, J.

LITIGATION - FRIVOLOUS
L3.92
Good Lord, what madness rules in brainsick men,
When for so slight and frivolous a cause
Such factious emulations shall arise!
1 Henry VI - IV i

LITIGATION, JOYS OF
L3.96
['T]is the sport to have the enginer
Hoist with his own petar
Hamlet III iv

"Careful and sagacious counseling should act as a prophylactic so that an overreaching and obdurate plaintiff ... does not run [this] risk." Brown, J. in Adams v. Peterson, 625 N.E. 2d 575, 576 (Mass. 1994).

LITIGATION - TURNING TABLES
L4.02
Why do we hold our tongues,
That most may claim this argument for ours?
Macbeth II iii

LITIGATION - WHEN OPPOSING SIDE IS SEEN AS TRANSGRESSING
L4.04
I shall break that merry sconce of yours.
Comedy of Errors I ii

LITIGATOR IN LOVE
L4.06
[N]ow,—instead of mounting barbed steeds
To fright the souls of fearful adversaries,—
He capers nimbly in a lady's chamber
To the lascivious pleasing of a lute.
Richard III - I i

LITIGATORS

L4.08

We are but warriors for the working-day
Henry V - IV iii

L4.10

I wear not
My dagger in my mouth.
Cymbeline IV ii

L4.12

[H]e does it with a better grace, but I do it
more natural.
Twelfth Night II iii

L4.14

In peace there's nothing so becomes a man
As modest stillness and humility:
But when the blast of war blows in our ears,
Then imitate the action of the tiger;
Stiffen the sinews, summon up the blood,
Disguise fair nature with hard-favour'd rage;
Then lend the eye a terrible aspect ...
Now set the teeth and stretch the nostril wide,
Hold hard the breath and bend up every spirit
To his full height.
Henry V - III i

LITIGATORS - AFTER WINNING TRIAL

L4.16

O, such a day,
So fought, so follow'd, and so fairly won,
Came not till now to dignify the times,
Since Caesar's fortunes!
2 Henry IV - I i

LITIGATORS - CREED
L4.18
King Richard: [L]ions make leopards tame.
Norfolk: Yea, but not change his spots.
Richard II - I i

LITIGATORS - EGO
L4.20
Doubt not ... they shall be well oppos'd.
1 Henry IV - IV iv

LITIGATORS IN CONVERSATION
L4.22
The bitter clamour of two eager tongues
Richard II - I i

LITIGATORS - PARANOIA
L4.24
Work, work your thoughts, and therein see a siege
Henry V - III Prologue

LITIGATORS - UPON THREATENING TO APPEAL
L4.26
I do see the bottom of Justice Shallow.
2 Henry IV - III ii

LITIGATORS - VIEW OF COURT CLERKS
L4.28
I did never know so full a voice issue from so empty a heart: but the saying is true,—the empty vessel makes the greatest sound.
Henry V - IV iv

LITIGATORS - WHEN THEY LOSE A CASE
L4.30
[F]or it comes to pass oft that a terrible oath, with a swaggering accent sharply twanged off, gives manhood more approbation than ever proof itself would have earned him.
Twelfth Night III iv

LITIGATORS WITHOUT A SENSE OF HUMOR
L4.32
[O]ur argument
Is all too heavy to admit much talk.
2 Henry IV - V ii

LITIGATORS - WOMEN
L4.34
O tiger's heart wrapt in a woman's hide!
3 Henry VI - I iv

THE LITIGIOUS ERA
L4.36
An age of discord and continual strife
1 Henry VI - V v

L4.40
We were not born to sue
Richard II - I i

LOBBYING
L4.44
[S]hall we now
Contaminate our fingers with base bribes
Julius Caesar IV iii

L4.46

I do not care: I'll give thrice so much ...
To any well-deserving friend.
1 Henry IV - III i

See also Yankwich, J. in U.S. v. Jones, 176 F. 2d 278, 290 (1949).

L4.48
Bidding the law make
court'sy to their will
Measure for Measure II iv

LOCAL REPRESENTATIVE TO ABA

L4.54

[M]y office is to noise abroad
2 Henry IV - Induction

LOGIC, A LAWYER'S
L4.58
Nothing that is so is so.
Twelfth Night IV i

LOSING PARTY – ATTORNEY'S FEES
L4.64
Your cause of sorrow
Must not be measured by his worth, for then
It hath no end.
Macbeth V viii

M

MAGISTRATES, UNITED STATES
M1.02
O that you could turn your eyes toward the napes of your necks, and make but an interior survey of your good selves! ... Why, then you should discover a brace of unmeriting, proud, violent, testy magistrates, alias fools ... You wear out a good wholesome forenoon in hearing a cause between an orange-wife and a fosset-seller; and then rejourn the controversy of three pence to a second day of audience. When you are hearing a matter between party and party, if you chance to be pinched with the colic, you make faces like mummers; set up the bloody flag against all patience; and, in roaring for a chamber-pot, dismiss the controversy bleeding, the more entangled by your hearing. All the peace you make in their cause is calling both the parties knaves.
Coriolanus II i

MAJORITY OPINION
M1.04
Believe my words,
For they are certain and unfallible.
1 Henry VI - I ii

MAJORITY RULE

M1.08

Son: What is a traitor?

Lady MacDuff: Why, one that swears and lies.

Son: And be all traitors that do so?

Lady MacDuff: Every one that does so is a traitor, and must be hanged.

Son: And must they all be hanged that swear and lie?

Lady MacDuff: Every one.

Son: Who must hang them?

Lady MacDuff: Why, the honest men.

Son: Then the liars and swearers are fools, for there are liars and swearers enow to beat the honest men and hang up them.

Macbeth IV ii

MAKING A FEDERAL CASE OF IT

M1.12

Sir Hugh, persuade me not; I will make
A Star Chamber matter of it.
Merry Wives of Windsor I i

MALUM PROHIBITUM AND MALUM IN SE

M1.20

Every offence is not a hate at first.
Merchant of Venice IV i

M1.24

We have strict statutes and most biting laws.
Measure for Measure I iii

M1.28

It is the law, not I, condemn your brother
Measure for Measure II ii

MALUM PROHIBITUM (CONT.)

M1.32
Tarry, Jew:
The law hath yet another hold on you...
It is enacted in the laws of Venice,
If it be proved against an alien
That by direct or indirect attempts
He seek the life of any citizen,
The party 'gainst the which he doth contrive
Shall seize one half his goods; the other half
Comes to the privy coffer of the state;
And the offender's life lies in the mercy
Of the Duke only, 'gainst all other voice.
Merchant of Venice IV i

MANAGING PARTNERS
M1.36
Uneasy lies the head that wears a crown.
2 Henry IV - III i

See Shakespeare and the Legal Process by J.D.E., 61 Virginia
Law Rev. 390, 392 (1975) for the limitations in singling
out legal matters in Shakespeare.

MARBURY v MADISON

M1.40
Stay!
Where's your commission, lords? words cannot carry
Authority so weighty.
Henry VIII - III ii

M1.44
Have you a precedent
Of this commission? I believe, not any.
We must not rend our subjects from our laws,
And stick them in our will.
Henry VIII - I ii

MENTAL CAPACITY

M1.48
But age, with his stealing steps,
Hath claw'd me in his clutch
Hamlet V i

Jackson v. Henninger, 482 S.W. 2d 323, 326 (Texas 1972). Shannon, J.

MENTAL ILLNESS

M1.52
Make mad the guilty and appal the free,
Confound the ignorant, and amaze indeed
The very faculties of eyes and ears.
Hamlet II ii

See State Farm v. Wicka, 474 N.W. 2d 324, 327 (Minn. 1991) as to
the general skepticism and disbelief as to mental illness. Gardebring, J.

MERCY

M1.56

No ceremony that to great ones 'longs,
Not the king's crown, nor the deputed sword,
The marshal's truncheon, nor the judge's robe,
Become them with one half so good a grace
As mercy does.

Measure for Measure II ii

Wollman v. Gross, 637 F. 2d 544, 550 (1980). Adams, J. dissents and
uses this cite to distinguish the spirit of the law from the letter of the
law.

M1.60

'Tis mightiest in the mightiest: it becomes
The throned monarch better than his crown ...
But mercy is above this sceptred sway;
It is enthroned in the hearts of kings,
It is an attribute to God himself

Merchant of Venice IV i

Perales v. Casillas, 903 F. 2d 1043, 1053 (1990). This excerpt is the
entire dissent of Goldberg, J.

MERGERS AND ACQUISITION LAWYER

M1.64

[N]ew created
The creatures that were mine, I say, or changed 'em,
Or else new form'd 'em; having both the key
Of officer and office, set all hearts
To what tune pleased his ear

The Tempest I ii

MILLION DOLLAR VERDICT CLUB

M1.68

O, I am fortune's fool.

Romeo & Juliet III i

MIRANDA RULE

M1.72

Miranda: Alack, what trouble
        Was I then to you!
Prospero: ... Thou wast that did preserve me.
The Tempest I ii

M1.74

Relate your wrongs: in what? by whom? be brief
Measure for Measure V i

MONEY TALKS

M1.76

Now, trust me, were it not against our laws,
Against my crown, my oath, my dignity,
Which princes, would they, may not disannul,
My soul should sue as advocate for thee.
But, though thou art adjudged to the death
And passed sentence may not be recall'd
But to our honour's great disparagement,
Yet I will favour thee in what I can.
Therefore, merchant, I'll limit thee this day
To seek thy life by beneficial help;
Try all the friends thou hast in Ephesus;
Beg thou, or borrow, to make up the sum,
And live; if no, then thou art doom'd to die.
Gaoler, take him to thy custody.
Comedy of Errors I i

MOOT COURT BRIEF
M1.78
[T]hey aim at it,
And botch the words up fit to their own thoughts
Hamlet IV v

MOOT COURT JUDGE TO PARTICIPANTS
M1.80
A fine volley of words, gentlemen, and
quickly shot of
Two Gentlemen of Verona II iv

MOTIONS, FILING UNTIMELY
M1.82
Our decrees,
Dead to infliction, to themselves are dead,
And liberty plucks justice by the nose.
Measure for Measure I iii

Conn. General v. Chicago Title, 690 F. 2d 115, 116 (1982). Posner, J. comes down hard on a lawyer whose motions were untimely filed.

MUCH ADO ABOUT NOTHING
M1.84
See ACLU v. Westmoreland, 323 F. Supp. 1153, 1155 (1971). Austin, J.

MUNICIPAL BOND SPECIALISTS
M1.86
[T]hey pray continually to their saint, the commonwealth; or rather, not pray to her, but prey on her, for
they ride up and down on her and make her their
boots.
1 Henry IV - II i

MURDER

M1.92

Murder most foul, as in the best it is;
But this most foul, strange, and unnatural.

Hamlet I v

This is the opening line of People v. Brown, 7 Cal. Rptr. 2d 370, 371 (1992). Crosby, J.

MURDER, ATTEMPTED - JURY'S VIEWPOINT

M1.98

The attempt and not the deed
Confounds us.

Macbeth II ii

N

NATIONAL REPORTER SYSTEM
N1.02
They have been at a great feast of languages, and
stolen the scraps.
Love's Labour's Lost V i

NATURAL LAW
N1.08
In nature's infinite book of secrecy
A little I can read
Antony & Cleopatra I ii

NEW YORK LOBBYISTS
N1.14
[L]ife is a shuttle.
Merry Wives of Windsor V i

See Eastern Air Lines v. N.Y. Air Lines, 559 F. Supp. 1270, 1275
(1983). Pollack, J.

NOT GUILTY
N1.20
Since what I am to say must be but that
Which contradicts my accusation and
The testimony on my part no other
But what comes from myself, it shall scarce boot me
To say "Not guilty." Mine integrity,
Being counted falsehood, shall, as I express it,
Be so received. But thus: if powers divine
Behold our human actions, as they do,
I doubt not then but innocence shall make
False accusation blush and tyranny
Tremble at patience.
Winter's Tale III ii

O

OATHS

O1.00

An oath is of no moment, being not took
Before a true and lawful magistrate,
That hath authority over him that swears ...
Your oath, my lord, is vain and frivolous.
3 Henry VI - I ii

O1.02

Let us once lose our oaths to find ourselves,
Or else we lose ourselves to keep our oaths.
Love's Labour's Lost IV iii

OFFICE ADMINISTRATOR

O1.04

Do your offices, do your offices
2 Henry IV - II i

OPENING ARGUMENT

O1.06

Unless my study and my books be false,
The argument you held was wrong in you
1 Henry VI - II iv

O1.08

Further I say—and further will maintain
Upon his bad life to make all this good,—
That he did plot the Duke of Gloucester's death;
Suggest his soon-believing adversaries,
And consequently, like a traitor coward,
Sluic'd out his innocent soul through streams of blood:
Which blood, like sacrificing Abel's, cries,

Even from the tongueless caverns of the earth,
To me for justice and rough chastisement;
And, by the glorious worth of my descent,
This arm shall do it, or this life be spent!
Richard II - I i

OPENING ARGUMENT - PRO SE
01.10
Pity me not but lend thy serious hearing to what I
shall unfold.
Hamlet I v

OPENING TO THE JURY
01.12
[T]his strange eventful history...
As You Like It II vii

OPPOSING COUNSEL
01.14
The mirror of all courtesy
Henry VIII -II i

OPPOSING COUNSEL'S WITNESS
O1.18
[A] tale
Told by an idiot, full of sound and fury,
Signifying nothing.
Macbeth V v

McNeill v. Butz, 480 F. 2d 314, 323 (1973). Winter, J.

ORAL ARGUMENT
O1.20
Speak the speech ... trippingly on the tongue
Hamlet III ii

O1.22
He draweth out the thread of his verbosity finer than
the staple of his argument.
Love's Labour's Lost V i

O1.28
[T]o what end are all these words?
Taming of the Shrew I ii

O1.32
Windy attorneys to their client woes,
Airy succeeders of intestate joys,
Poor breathing orators of miseries!
Let them have scope: though what they do impart
Help not at all, yet do they ease the heart.
Richard III - IV iv

O1.36
My words fly up, my thoughts remain below.
Words without thoughts never to heaven go.
Hamlet III iii

P

PARADISE OR HELL
P1.02
When every case in law is right:
No squire in debt, nor no poor knight;
When slanders do not live in tongues;
Nor cutpurses come not to throngs.
King Lear III ii

PARALEGALS
P1.04
Life's but a walking shadow
Macbeth V v

For an interesting collection of quotations on the value of life, see The
Kekoskee, 47 F. 2d 235, 237 (1931). Neterer, J.

PARDONS
P1.08
The quality of mercy is not strain'd,
It droppeth as the gentle rain from heaven
Upon the place beneath: it is twice blest;
It blesseth him that gives and him that takes
'Tis mightiest in the mightiest: it becomes
The throned monarch better than his crown;
His sceptre shows the force of temporal power,
The attribute to awe and majesty,
Wherein doth sit the dread and fear of kings;
But mercy is above this sceptred sway;
It is enthroned in the hearts of kings,
It is an attribute to God himself;
And earthly power doth then show likest God's
When mercy seasons justice.
Merchant of Venice IV i

Much quoted. See Posner, J., In re Frelich, 894 F. 2d 881, 886 (1989).

P1.14
[W]e may pity, though
not pardon thee.
Comedy of Errors I i

PARTNER, ADVICE TO NEWLY MADE
P1.24
This have I thought good to deliver thee, my dearest
partner of greatness, that thou mightest not lose the
dues of rejoicing by being ignorant of what greatness
is promised thee.
Macbeth I v 11

PARTNER - OBITUARY
P1.26
Nothing in his life
Became him like the leaving of it.
Macbeth I iv

PARTNER'S ADVICE TO YOUNG ASSOCIATE
P1.28
Mend your speech a little,
Lest it may mar your fortunes
King Lear I i 96

PARTNER'S SHARE
P1.32
Bolingbroke: My gracious Lord, I come but for mine
       own ...
    As my true service shall deserve ...
Richard: Well you deserve: they well deserve to have
    That know the strong'st and surest way to get.
Richard II - III iii

PARTNERS - ASSOCIATES' VIEW
P1.40
[T]hou variest no more from picking of purses than
giving direction doth from labouring.
1 Henry IV - II i

PARTNERS - EVALUATING ASSOCIATES
P1.44
He who the sword of heaven will bear
Should be as holy as severe; ...
Shame to him whose cruel striking
Kills for faults of his own liking!
Measure for Measure III ii

PARTNERS - RETIREMENT

P1.48

[’T]is our fast intent
To shake all cares and business from our age;
Conferring them on younger strengths, while we
Unburden'd crawl toward death.

King Lear I i

"The result is predictable to those who recall King Lear." Cohn, J. in Marra v. Burgdorf Realtors, 726 F. Supp. 1000, 1002 (1989).

PARTNERSHIP

P1.52

[S]huffled off this mortal coil

Hamlet III i

P1.56
We are such stuff
As dreams are made on

The Tempest IV i

PARTNERSHIP (CONT.)

P1.60
O! that way madness lies
King Lear III iv

P1.64
Sweet partner,
I must not yet forsake you
Henry VIII - I iv

P1.70
[F]or aught that I could ever read,
Could ever hear by tale or history,
The course of true love never did run smooth
Midsummer Night's Dream I i
U.S. v. Polito, 856 F. 2d 414, 415 (1988). Selya, J.

PARTNERSHIP - BREAKING UP
P1.72
And whether we shall meet again I know not.
Therefore our everlasting farewell take: ...
If we do meet again, why, we shall smile;
If not, why then, this parting was well made.
Julius Caesar V i

PARTNERSHIP, LOSING OUT ON

P1.76

Men at some time are masters of their fates:
The fault, dear Brutus, is not in our stars,
But in ourselves
Julius Caesar I ii

Cole v. Erie Lackawanna Rwy., 396 F. Supp. 65, 68 (Ohio 1975).
Walinski, J.

P1.78

[W]hen Fortune means to men most good,
She looks upon them with a threat'ning eye.
King John III iv

U.S. v. Ingraham, 832 F. 2d 229, 230 (1987). Selya, J.

PARTNERSHIP MEETINGS

P1.80

[A] plague upon't when thieves cannot be true one
to another!
1 Henry IV - II ii

PARTNERSHIP - MERGER

P1.88

O brave new world,
That has such people in't!
The Tempest V i

PARTNERSHIP, TWO-PERSON

P1.92

One of these men is Genius to the other;
And so of these. Which is the natural man,
And which the spirit? Who deciphers them?
Comedy of Errors V i

PASSION – THE REASONABLE LAWYER'S APPROACH

P1.94

I do not seek to quench your love's hot fire
But qualify the fire's extreme rage,
Lest it should burn above the bounds of reason.
Two Gentlemen of Verona II vii

PATERNITY

P1.96

So, now I have confess'd that he is thine
Sonnet 184

PATERNITY SUITS

P2.02

It is a wise father that knows his own child.
Merchant of Venice II ii

PER CURIAM DECISION

P2.04

[A] wilful stillness entertain,
With purpose to be dress'd in an opinion
Of wisdom, gravity, profound conceit,
As who should say, "I am Sir Oracle,
And when I ope my lips let no dog bark!"
O my Antonio, I do know of these
That therefore only are reputed wise
For saying nothing
Merchant of Venice I i

PERJURY
P2.08
Glendower: Why, I can teach you, cousin, to command
    The devil.
Hotspur: And I can teach thee, coz, to shame the devil
    By telling truth: tell truth, and shame the devil.
1 Henry IV - III i

PERSONAL INJURY LAWYER'S PRAYER
P2.12
[A remedy for every] heartache and the thousand
    natural shocks
That flesh is heir to
Hamlet III i

But see Moore v. Regents, 271 Cal. Rptr. 146, 165 (1990). Arabian, J. dissenting. Cited in Miles v. Scripps, 810 F. Supp. 191, 197 (1993). Rhoades, J.

PLAIN MEANING RULE
P2.16
I pray thee, understand a plain man in his plain
meaning
Merchant of Venice III v

PLAINTIFF
P2.18
[Give] me justice, justice, justice, justice!
Measure for Measure V i

PLEA BARGAINING
P2.20
What say you? will you yield and this avoid,
Or, guilty in defence, be thus destroy'd?
Henry V - III iii

PLEA BARGAINING (CONT.)

P2.22

Davy (*to Justice Shallow*): I have served your worship truly, sir, this eight years; and if I cannot once or twice in a quarter bear out a knave against an honest man, I have but a very little credit with your worship. The knave is my honest friend, sir; therefore, I beseech your worship, let him be countenanced.

2 Henry IV - V i

See Bruneau, Shakespeare's Law, 17 McGill Law Jl. 792 (1971)

PLEADING POVERTY

P2.24

Sweet are the uses of adversity

As You Like It II i

P2.28

O, for my sake do you with Fortune chide,
The guilty goddess of my harmful deeds,
That did not better for my life provide
Than public means, which public manners breeds.

Sonnet 111

County of Oakland v. Detroit, 866 F. 2d 839, 843 (1989). Nelson, J.

POOR ARGUMENT

P2.32

I could have given less matter
A better ear.

Antony & Cleopatra II i

POOR LOSER

P2.36

I had rather see a wren hawk at a fly than this decision.

Two Noble Kinsmen V iii

See Marder, ed. Speak the Speech 87 (1994)

POSITIVE LAW

P2.40
Every subject's duty is the king's
Henry V - IV i

P2.44
[T]he force of temporal power
Merchant of Venice IV i

POSSESSION IS NINE-TENTHS OF THE LAW

P2.52
King John: Our strong possession and
our right for us.
Queen Elinor: Your strong possession
much more than your right
King John I i

POUND OF FLESH

P2.54
Merchant of Venice IV i

The danger of directing a comment of this type at a judge is spelled out in State v. Conliff, 401 N.E. 2d 469, 477 (1978). Whiteside, J. in dissent.

POWER OF ATTORNEY

P2.56
Flattering himself in project of a power
Much smaller than the smallest of his thoughts
2 Henry IV - I iii

P2.58
[T]ake with you free power to ratify,
Augment, or alter, as your wisdoms best
Shall see advantageable for our dignity
Henry V - V ii

PRECEDENT

P2.64
Portia: [T]here is no power in Venice
Can alter a decree established:
'Twill be recorded for a precedent,
And many an error, by the same example,
Will rush into the state: it cannot be.
Merchant of Venice IV i

See Rand v. State, 341 S.W. 2d 9, 13 (Ark. 1960). McFadden concurring. See also Davis v. Johnson [1979] A.C. 264.

P2.70
That that is is.
Twelfth Night IV ii

PRECEDENTS, FOLLOWING BAD
P2.72

The evil that men do lives after them;
The good is oft interred with their bones
Julius Caesar III ii

In Turner v. Consumers Pwr. Co., 136 N.W. 2d 1,3 (1965). Black, J. uses this quotation to express his regrets at having to follow a bad precedent.

PRENUPTIAL AGREEMENTS
P2.74

Petruchio: Then tell me, if I get your daughter's love,
    What dowry shall I have with her to wife?
Baptista: After my death the one half of my lands,
    And in possession twenty thousand crowns.
Petruchio: And, for that dowry, I'll assure her of
    Her widowhood, be it that she survive me,
    In all my lands and leases whatsoever:
    Let specialties be therefore drawn between us,
    That covenants may be kept on either hand.
Baptista: Ay, when the special thing is well obtain'd,
    That is, her love; for that is all in all.
Petruchio: Why, that is nothing
Taming of the Shrew II i

See Brooks v. Brooks, 733 P. 2d 1044, 1048 (Alaska 1987). Burke, J.

PRESIDENT - SIGNING INTO LAW
P2.76

So to the laws at large I write my name
Love's Labour's Lost I i

PRESS COVERAGE
P2.80

How every fool can play upon the word!
Merchant of Venice III v

PRE-TRIAL

P2.84

[S]o shall my anticipation prevent your discovery

Hamlet II ii

PRIMA FACIE PROOF

P2.88

Doth not the crown of England prove the King?

King John II i

PRISONERS - MISTREATMENT OF

P2.94

But that I am forbid

To tell the secrets of my prison-house,

I could a tale unfold whose lightest word

Would harrow up thy soul, freeze thy young blood

Hamlet I v

People v. Brown, 7 Cal. Rptr. 2d 370 (1992). Crosby, J.

PRISONS - ABOLITION OF

P3.02

I would we were all of one mind, and one mind good;

O, there were desolation of gaolers and gallowses!

I speak against my present profit, but my wish hath a
    preferment in't.

Cymbeline V iv

PRIVITY

P3.04

A comfortable doctrine, and much may be said of it.

Twelfth Night I v

PRO BONO CASES

P3.08

So shines a good deed in a naughty world.

Merchant of Venice V i

PRO BONO CASES - VIEW OF PAYING CLIENTS

P3.12

You pay a great deal too dear for what's given freely.

Winter's Tale I i

PRO SE

P3.20

Therein the patient
Must minister to himself.

Macbeth V iii

PROCESS

P3.24

Proceed by process

Coriolanus III i

PROFESSIONAL EXPERT

P3.28

If thou wert honourable,
Thou wouldst have told this tale for virtue, not
For such an end thou seek'st

Cymbeline I vi

PROSECUTION ARGUMENT FOR A LONG SENTENCE

P3.32

Brutus: Fashion it thus; that what he is ...
Would run to these and these extremities;
And therefore think him as a serpent's egg
Which, hatch'd, would, as his kind, grow
    mischievous,
And kill him in the shell.

Julius Caesar II i

PROSECUTORS - DATING

P3.36

[T]herefore was I created with a stubborn outside,
with an aspect of iron, that when I come to woo
ladies I fright them.

Henry V - V ii

PROSSER ON TORTS

P3.40

[A] book where men
May read strange matters.

Macbeth I v

PROTECTED WITNESS PROGRAM
P3.44
O heavens! that this treason were not,
or not I the detector!
King Lear III v

PROXIMATE CAUSE
P3.52
[F]ind out the cause of this effect,
Or rather say, the cause of this defect,
For this effect defective comes by cause.
Hamlet II ii

P3.56
There is occasions and causes why and wherefore
in all things
Henry V - V i

Q

QUALIFICATIONS FOR OFFICE
Q1.02
Yon Cassius has a lean and hungry look ... such men
are dangerous.
Julius Caesar I ii

Geary v. Renne, 911 F. 2d 280, 313 (1990). Alarcon, J. in dissent.

QUESTIONS FROM THE BENCH
Q1.08
Abraham: Do you bite your thumb at us, sir?
Sampson: Is the law of our side if I say ay?
Romeo & Juliet I i

QUESTIONS TO THE BENCH
Q1.14
Be now the father and propose a son,
Hear your own dignity so much profan'd,
See your most dreadful laws so loosely slighted,
Behold yourself so by a son disdain'd;
And then imagine me taking your part,
And in your power soft silencing your son:
After this cold considerance, sentence me
2 Henry IV - V ii

R

RAINMAKERS

R1.02
He wants nothing of a god but eternity and a heaven
to throne in.
Coriolanus V iv

R1.04
[A]t my birth
The frame and huge foundation of the earth
Shak'd like a coward.
1 Henry IV -III i

R1.06
The eagle suffers little birds to sing,
And is not careful what they mean thereby
Titus Andronicus IV iv

RAINMAKERS AS ROLE MODELS

R1.08
[T]hose that could speak low and tardily
Would turn their own perfection to abuse
To seem like him: so that in speech, in gait,
In diet, in affections of delight, ...
He was the mark and glass, copy and book,
That fashion'd others.
2 Henry IV - II iii

REAL ESTATE

R1.12
A little water clears us of this deed.
Macbeth II ii

State v. Shanahan, 404 A. 2d 975, 982 (Me. 1979). Wernick, J.

REAL ESTATE (CONT.)

R1.16
Now would I give a thousand furlongs of sea for an acre of barren ground
The Tempest I i

R1.20
Now does he feel his title
Hang loose about him, like a giant's robe
Upon a dwarfish thief.
Macbeth V ii

REAL ESTATE LAWYER

R1.22
Why, here he comes, swelling like a turkey-cock.
Henry V - V i

RECUSATION

R1.24
I do believe,
Induced by potent circumstances, that
You are mine enemy, and make my challenge
You shall not be my judge; for it is you
Have blown this coal betwixt my lord and me;
Which God's dew quench. Therefore I say again,
I utterly abhor, yea, from my soul
Refuse you for my judge; whom, yet once more,
I hold my most malicious foe, and think not
At all a friend to truth.
Henry VIII - II iv

See NLRB v. Baldwin Locomotive, 128 F. 2d 39, 52 (1942) in which Judge Clark concurred and dissented.

REFERRAL FEES

R1.28
[I]ndirection thereby grows direct
King John III i

See Associates Financial Services v. Johnson, 197 S.E. 2d 764, 766 (Ga. 1973). Eberhardt, J.

REFRESHING RECOLLECTION

R1.32
Purpose is but the slave to memory
Hamlet III ii

REGULATIONS

R1.36
Tomorrow and tomorrow and tomorrow creeps in this petty pace from day to day ... and all our yesterdays have lighted fools the way to dusty death.
Macbeth V v

REHABILITATION OF CRIMINALS

R1.40
To me it is a prison.
Hamlet II ii

REHEARINGS

R1.42
[A] good play needs no epilogue
As You Like It - Epilogue

R1.44
Sit down awhile;
And let us once again assail your ears,
That are so fortified against our story
Hamlet I i

REIT SALESMAN
R1.46
[Y]ou may buy land now as cheap
as stinking mackerel.
1 Henry IV - II iv

REMEDIES FOR SPECIFIC PROBLEM
R1.48
What need to bridge much broader than the flood?
The fairest grant is the necessity.
Look, what will serve is fit
Much Ado About Nothing I i

See James v. U.S., 760 F. 2d 590, 602 (1985). Reavley, J.

REQUEST FOR CONTINUANCE, RESPONSE TO

R1.56

Justice Shallow: I will not excuse you; you shall not be excused; excuses shall not be admitted; there is no excuse shall serve; you shall not be excused.

2 Henry IV - V i

RETAINERS

R1.60

O my ducats!

Merchant of Venice II vii

REVENUE ACTS

R1.64

And daily new exactions are devised,
As blanks, benovolences, and I wot not what:
But what, o' God's name, doth become of this?
Richard II - II i

RHETORIC IN COURT
R1.72
Sweet smoke of rhetoric!
Love's Labour's Lost III i

R1.76
In law, what plea so tainted and corrupt
But, being season'd with a gracious voice,
Obscures the show of evil?
Merchant of Venice III ii

The opening line of concurring opinion in McCauley v. State, 405 So.
2d 1350, 1351 (Fla 1981). Cowart, J.

RIGHT TO COUNSEL
R1.84
What would you have me do? I am a subject,
And I challenge law: attorneys are denied me
Richard II - II iii

ROBERT'S RULES OF ORDER
R1.88
Justice Shallow: The Council shall hear it; it is a riot.
Sir Hugh Evans: It is not meet the Council hear a riot;
    there is no fear of Got in a riot; the Council, look
    you, shall desire to hear the fear of Got, and not
    to hear a riot
Merry Wives of Windsor I i

RULE AGAINST PERPETUITIES
R1.92
The valiant never taste of death but once.
Of all the wonders that I yet have heard,
It seems to me most strange that men should fear;
Seeing that death, a necessary end,
Will come when it will come.
Julius Caesar II ii

RULE OF LAW

R1.96

Chief Justice: Sweet princes, what I did, I did
      in honour,
  Led by the impartial conduct of my soul:
  And never shall you see that I will beg
  A ragged and forestall'd remission.
  If truth and upright innocency fail me,
  I'll to the King my master that is dead,
  And tell him who hath sent me after him ...
King Henry: You all look strangely on me:
      and you most; (*to the Chief Justice*)
  You are, I think, assured I love you not.
Chief Justice: I am assured, if I be measured rightly,
  Your Majesty hath no just cause to hate me.
King Henry: No!
  How might a prince of my great hopes forget
  So great indignities you laid upon me?
  What! rate, rebuke, and roughly send to prison
  The immediate heir of England! Was this easy?
  May this be wash'd in Lethe, and forgotten?
Chief Justice: I then did use the person of
      your father;
  The image of his power lay then in me:
  And, in the administration of his law,
  Whiles I was busy for the commonwealth,
  Your Highness pleased to forget my place,
  The majesty and power of law and justice,
  The image of the King whom I presented,
  And struck me in my very seat of judgement;
  Whereon, as an offender to your father,
  I gave bold way to my authority
  And did commit you. If the deed were ill,
  Be you contented, wearing now the garland,
  To have a son set your decrees at nought,

To pluck down justice from your awful bench,
To trip the course of law and blunt the sword
That guards the peace and safety of your person;
Nay, more, to spurn at your most royal image
And mock your workings in a second body.
2 Henry IV - V ii

SCOFFLAW
S1.02
There cannot be those numberless offences
'Gainst me, that I cannot take peace with.
Henry VIII - II i

SECOND OFFENDERS
S1.06
It will help me nothing
To plead mine innocence; for that dye is on me
Which makes my whitest part black.
Henry VIII - I i

SENATORIAL COURTESY
S1.12
Brabantio: Thou art a villain.
Iago: You are—a senator.
Othello I i

SENIOR PARTNERS - FAME
S1.20
He was famous, sir, in his profession,
And it was his great right to be so
All's Well That Ends Well I i

SENIOR YEAR IN COLLEGE
S1.28
To be, or not to be: that is the question.
Hamlet III i

See Sisk v. Williamson County, 632 N.E. 2d 672, 678 (Ill. 1994),
where Judge Lewis considers the issue, "to mow or not to mow." See
also 80 Minn. Law Rev. 1615 (1996).

SETTLING A CASE
S1.40
A peace is of the nature of a conquest;
For then both parties nobly are subdued,
And neither party loser.
2 Henry IV - IV ii

SLANDER
S1.48
No, 'tis slander,
Whose edge is sharper than the sword
Cymbeline III iv

SMALL CLAIMS
S1.52
Fang: Sir John, I arrest you at the suit of Mistress
      Quickly ...

Falstaff: Away, you scullion! you rampallian! you
      fustilarian! I'll tickle your catastrophe.

Chief Justice: What is the matter? keep the peace here, ho! ...

Mistress Quickly: [H]e is arrested at my suit.

Chief Justice: For what sum?

Mistress Quickly: It is more than for some, my lord; it is for all, all I have. He hath eaten me out of house and home; he hath put all my substance into that fat belly of his ...

Falstaff: What is the gross sum that I owe thee?

Mistress Quickly: Marry, if thou were an honest man, thyself and the money too. Thou didst swear to me upon a parcel-gilt goblet ... to marry me and make me my lady thy wife ... I put thee now to thy book-oath: deny it, if thou canst.

2 Henry IV - II i

SOCRATIC METHOD - PROFESSOR'S VIEW

S1.58
Read, and declare the meaning.
Cymbeline V v

S1.62
I would that you would answer me.
1 Henry VI - V iii

S1.66
To punish you by the heels would amend the attention of your ears
2 Henry IV - I ii

SOCRATIC METHOD - STUDENT'S VIEW

S1.70
You'll rue the time
That clogs me with this answer.
Macbeth III vi

SOCRATIC METHOD - STUDENTS (CONT.)

S1.76
[M]y thoughts are ripe in mischief
Twelfth Night V i

S1.80
O happy torment, when my torturer
Doth teach me answers for deliverance!
Merchant of Venice III ii

SPECIFIC PERFORMANCE

S1.84
Whereof the execution did cry out
Against the non-performance
Winter's Tale I ii

SPEEDY TRIAL - REQUEST FOR

S1.88
It issues from the rancour of a villain,
A recreant and most degenerate traitor:
Which in myself I boldly will defend;
And interchangeably hurl down my gage
Upon this overweening traitor's foot,
To prove myself a loyal gentleman
Even in the best blood chamber'd in his bosom.
In haste whereof, most heartily I pray
Your Highness to assign our trial day.
Richard II - I i

S1.92
If it were done when 'tis done, then 'twere well
It were done quickly.
Macbeth I vii

STAR CHAMBER
S1.96
Masking the business from the common eye
For sundry weighty reasons.
Macbeth III i

STARE DECISIS
S2.02
The time has been
That, when the brains were out, the man would die,
And there an end; but now they rise again,
With twenty mortal murders on their crowns,
And push us from our stools.
Macbeth III iv

Cited in Western Coal & Mining v. Hilvert, 160 P. 2d 331, 334 (Ariz. 1945), in reference to the appeal process.

S2.04
Out of this nettle, danger, we pluck this flower, safety
1 Henry IV - II iii

STARE DECISIS (CONT.)

S2.08
Which, unreversed, stands in effectual force
Two Gentlemen of Verona III i

STATUTES-AT-LARGE

S2.16
[L]aws for all faults,
But faults so countenanced, that the strong statutes
Stand like the forfeits in a barbershop,
As much in mock as mark.
Measure for Measure V i

STATUTORY INTERPRETATION

S2.24
Confusion now hath made his masterpiece!
Macbeth II iii

Attorney General v. Waldron, 426 A. 2d 929, 941 (Md. 1981).
Digges, J. applies this to the equal protection clause.

S2.32
Let not the cloud of sorrow justle [the language]
From what it purpos'd
Love's Labour's Lost V i

For an application to trust law, see Equitable Life v. Porter-Englehart,
867 F.2d 79 (1989), Selya, J.

SUBPOENAS

S2.40
A heavy summons lies like lead upon me
Macbeth II i

SUBPOENAS (CONT.)

S2.48
[U]nbidden guests
Are often welcomest when they are gone.
1 Henry VI - II ii

SUMMER ASSOCIATES - FIRST DAY OF WORK

S2.56
All furnish'd, all in arms;
All plum'd like estridges that wing the wind;
Bated like eagles having lately bath'd;
Glittering in golden coats, like images;
As full of spirit as the month of May,
And gorgeous as the sun at midsummer;
Wanton as youthful goats, wild as young bulls.
1 Henry IV - IV i

SUNSHINE LAWS
S2.60
Light seeking light doth light of light beguile
Love's Labour's Lost I i

SUPREME COURT - SPLIT DECISION
S2.64
Thrice to thine and thrice to mine
And thrice again, to make up nine.
Macbeth I iii

SUPREME COURT JUSTICE
S2.70
['T]is a burden
Too heavy for a man that hopes for heaven!
Henry VIII - III ii

T

TAKEOVER - VIEW OF COUNSEL TO THE TAKEN OVER
T1.02
Company, villainous company, hath been the spoil of me.
1 Henry IV - III iii

TAKINGS
T1.04
You take my house when you do take the prop
That doth sustain my house; you take my life
When you do take the means whereby I live.
Merchant of Venice IV i

TAX COMMISSIONER'S LAMENT
T1.08
I tax not you, you elements
King Lear III ii

TAX LAWYERS
T1.12
O, he is as tedious
As a tired horse, a railing wife;
Worse than a smoky house
1 Henry IV - III i

TAXATION - APRIL 15
T1.18
What has this day deserved? What hath it done,
That it in golden letters should be set
Among the high tides in the calendar?
King John III i

TAXATION - DISCOVERY REQUESTS BY IRS

T1.24

When we grow stronger, then we'll make our claim:
Till then, 'tis wisdom to conceal our meaning.

3 Henry VI - IV vii

TEACHING CONSTITUTIONAL LAW

T2.02

But in these cases
We still have judgement here; that we but teach
Bloody instructions, which being taught, return
To plague the inventor. This even-handed justice
Commends the ingredients of our poison'd chalice
To our own lips.

Macbeth I vii

TEMPORARY INSANITY

T2.08

I am but mad north-north-west.
When the wind is southerly I know a hawk from a
    handsaw.

Hamlet II ii

In re Erickson, 815 F. 2d 1090, 1092 (1987). Easterbrook, J.
discusses the feigning of madness.

TESTIMONY OF OPPOSITION'S
STAR WITNESS

T2.14

[T]he rankest compound of villainous smell that ever
offended nostril.

Merry Wives of Windsor III v

TESTIMONY OF OPPOSITION'S STAR WITNESS (CONT.)

T2.20

And in the porches of my ears did pour
The leperous distilment; whose effect
Holds such an enmity with blood of man
That swift as quicksilver it courses through
The natural gates and alleys of the body,
And with a sudden vigour it doth posset
And curd, like eager droppings into milk,
The thin and wholsome blood. So did it mine:
And a most instant tetter bark'd about,
Most lazar-like, with vile and loathsome crust,
All my smooth body. ...
O, horrible! O, horrible! most horrible!
Hamlet I v

THREE-JUDGE APPELLATE COURT

T2.26

When shall we three meet again
In thunder, lightning, or in rain?
Macbeth I i

THROWING IN THE TOWEL

T2.32

It boots not to resist both wind and tide.
3 Henry VI - IV iii

TIMESHEETS, FILLING OUT

T2.38

[H]e weighs time
Even to the utmost grain
Henry V - II iv

TIMESHEETS, FILLING OUT (CONT.)
T2.40
I do count the clock that tells the time
Sonnet 12

T2.44
[N]ow hath time made me his numbering clock:
My thoughts are minutes.
Richard II - V v

TOO GOOD AN ARGUMENT
T2.48
Well have you argu'd, sir; and, for your pains,
Of capital treason we arrest you here.
Richard II - IV i

TORTS LAWYER TO CLIENT
T2.50
Your suit's unprofitable; stand up, I say.
Measure for Measure V i

TOUGH CASES
T2.52
Longaville: O, some authority how to proceed;
 Some tricks, some quillets, how to cheat the devil.
Dumain: Some salve for perjury.
Love's Labour's Lost IV iii

TRADE SECRETS
T2.56
That false villain
Whom I employ'd was preemploy'd by him.
He has discover'd my design.
Winter's Tale II i

TRADEMARKS

T2.60

A right fair mark, fair coz, is soonest hit.

Romeo & Juliet I i

TRIAL - THE GALLERY

T2.64

A thousand blushing apparitions

Much Ado About Nothing IV i

TRUSTS

T2.72

'Tis in reversion that I do possess;
But what it is, that is not yet known; what
I cannot name; 'tis nameless woe, I wot.

Richard II - II ii

TRUSTS AND ESTATES

T2.80

[A] man can die but once

2 Henry IV - III ii

See Selya, J. in R.. Higher Educ. v. Sec'y, U.S. Dept of Edu., 929 F. 2d 844, 854 (1991)

TRUSTS AND ESTATES - CLIENT'S VIEW OF LAWYER

T3.02

He was a gentleman on whom I built
An absolute trust.

Macbeth I iv

TRUSTS AND ESTATES - CLIENT'S VIEW OF LAWYER (CONT.)
T3.04
There's a divinity that shapes our ends,
Rough-hew them how we will
Hamlet V ii

People v. Martin, 192 N.W. 2d 215, 219 (1971). Adams, J. on criminal insanity.

TRUSTS AND ESTATES LAWYERS
T3.06
Let's talk of graves, of worms and epitaphs;
Make dust our paper ...
Let's choose executors and talk of wills
Richard II - III ii

T3.08
Death, death: O amiable lovely death!
King John III iv

TRUSTS AND ESTATES - WORDS OF CONSOLATION
T3.12
[N]o legacy is so rich as honesty.
All's Well That Ends Well III v

TRYING A CASE - ADVICE
T3.14
Heat not a furnace for your foe so hot
That it do singe yourself. We may outrun,
By violent swiftness, that which we run at,
And lose by over-running.
Henry VIII - I i

TRYING IN ABSENTIA
T3.16
Thieves are not judged [unless] they are by to hear,
Although apparent guilt be seen in them
Richard II - IV i

TWELFTH AMENDMENT
T3.18
What is the city but the people?
Coriolanus III i

TWO-LAWYER FIRMS

T3.20

Never so few, and never yet more need.

2 Henry IV - I i

U

UNBILLABLE HOURS
U1.02
The noisome weeds, which without profit suck
The soil's fertility from wholesome flowers.
Richard II - III iv

U1.04
Words pay no debts
Troilus & Cressida III ii

UNCONSCIONABILITY
U1.06
The pound of flesh which I demand of him,
Is dearly bought, 'tis mine, and I will have it.
If you deny me, fie upon your law!
Merchant of Venice IV i

UNIFORM STATE LAWS
U1.08
The unity and married calm of states
Troilus & Cressida I iii

USURY
U1.16
He hates our sacred nation, and he rails,
Even there where merchants most do congregate,
On me, my bargains, and my well-won thrift,
Which he calls interest
Merchant of Venice I iii

Cited in Riggs Natl. Bank v. D.C., 581 A. 2d 1229, 1253 (1990) in a case involving escheat. Schwelb, J.

VALUATION

V1.02

Troilus: What aught is but as 'tis valued?
Hector: But value dwells not in particular will;
    It holds his estimate and dignity
    As well wherein 'tis precious of itself
    As in the prizer

Troilus & Cressida II ii

W

WALL STREET LAWYER
W1.02
Knowest me not by my clothes?
Cymbeline IV ii

WITNESS
W1.08
His heart is fracted and corroborate.
Henry V - II i

WITNESS - BEFORE BEING STOPPED BY AN OBJECTION

W1.12

And thereby hangs a tale. . .

As You Like It II vii

WITNESSES

W1.16

There is no terror, Cassius, in your threats,
For I am arm'd so strong in honesty
That they pass by me as the idle wind,
Which I respect not.

Julius Caesar IV iii

W1.20

To show an unfelt sorrow is an office
Which the false man does easy.

Macbeth II iii

W.122

Ask me what question thou canst possible,
And I will answer unpremeditated

1 Henry VI - I ii

W1.24

[W]hat you speak is in your conscience wash'd
As pure as sin with baptism.

Henry V - I ii

W1.28

[T]ongue-tied in their guiltiness.

Julius Caesar I i

WITNESSES (CONT.)

W1.32

Come, sit down, every mother's son, and rehearse your parts.

Midsummer Night's Dream III i

WITNESSES - ADVICE TO

W1.36

Virtue is bold, and goodness never fearful.

Measure for Measure III i

W1.40

Be not thy tongue thy own shame's orator

Comedy of Errors III ii

WOMEN LAWYERS

W1.46

I will make
One of her women lawyer to me, for
I yet not understand the case myself.

Cymbeline II iii

W1.52

[A] woman's voice may do some good,
When articles too nicely urg'd be stood on.

Henry V - V ii

WORKAHOLIC LAWYERS, RESPONSE TO

W1.56

I dare do all that may become a man;
Who dares do more is none.

Macbeth I vii

INDEX